WINE. all the time.

the casual guide
to confident drinking

MARISSA A.
ROSS

A PLUME BOOK

PLUME
An imprint of Penguin Random House LLC
375 Hudson Street
New York, New York 10014

LIBRARY OF CONGRESS CATALOGING-IN-PUBLICATION DATA
has been applied for.

ISBN 9780399574160

Printed in the United States of America
1   3   5   7   9   10   8   6   4   2

Book design by Sabrina Bowers

To my husband, Benjamin

Contents

WINE. all the time.

MELITA —
I KNOW YOU DON'T
HAVE A FAVORITE
WINE (<u>YET</u>!) BUT
I THINK IT MIGHT
BE GAMAY? FINGERS
CROSSED!
CHEERS!
♥ Marissa Ross

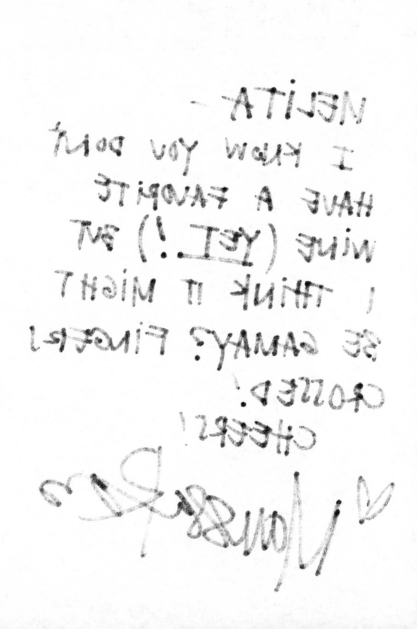

Introduction

I'm just going to get this out of the way: I am **not** a sommelier. People always assume that I am when they learn I'm a wine columnist, and I don't blame them. Those are two very logical dots to connect, like A to B or Nate Dogg to Mr. Warren G. No one hears that I'm a wine columnist and is like, *"Oh, shit! So you must be a college-dropout comedy writer, then!"* Being a college-dropout-comedy-writer-turned-wine-columnist doesn't have quite the same ring to it as *saw-muhl-yay*, but on the bright side, I didn't have to take any tests to earn the title and people can actually pronounce it. The important thing to take away from this is that despite my lack of formal education in this world, it eventually led me to writing the book you now hold in your hands: an unconventional, unpretentious guide to wine that I hope will help you become a more confident, more adventurous drinker.

Because you don't need to be a sommelier to know your way around wine. That notion is as insane as telling someone they need to go to film school to have a good time at the movies. Sure, it helps if you're interested in directing Scorsese-style tracking shots one day, but you don't have to be top of your class at NYU with a brand-new beret to be entertained by *Goodfellas*. And yet, we've all been made to feel that way about wine at one point or another, whether it's been while browsing the shelves of a stuffy wine shop, being side-eyed at a dinner party for throwing some ice in your Sauv Blanc, or being winesplained by your hard-liner in-law.

Wine is for everyone, and anyone can learn about it. It isn't this sacred subject surmountable by only a handful of human aroma indexes. That might be true if you're trying to sniff out specific French slopes in glasses of Sémillon, but most people out there are just trying to find a reasonably priced Pinot Noir. And for that, you do not need to know "everything." You need to know the basics of tasting, so you can describe what you like. You need to know the basics of how wine is made and the effects of regions, so you can recognize patterns in the wines you like. And you need to know the basics of buying wine, so you can buy more of those wines you like, instead of shopping with your fingers crossed. This may seem like a lot right now, but you can totally do it. I know this because I totally did it.

When I started off my writing career, I was a blogger with a reputation as a freewheeling wino with a proclivity for cursing and little regard for open-container laws. When Molly McAleer started HelloGiggles in 2011, she suggested I do a video series reviewing all the shitty wines I drank. Thus, *Wine Time* was born, "the show where a woman who has absolutely no qualifications to be reviewing wine, aside from the fact that she drinks it every day, reviews wine." I studied the steps of tasting and approached each wine like it was a $200 unicorn bottle rather than a $2 dusty bottle from House of Spirits. I inspected the color and clarity, swirled and assessed the bouquet, took three sips, and then I chugged it, a step I declared "the Ross Test."

After ten episodes of reviewing wines under $10, I came to the conclusion that all wines under $10 tasted like all other wines under $10. I was bored, but thirsty for more. I had never thought of tasting wines before *Wine Time*, and suddenly that was all I could think about. Rather than just chugging to get drunk, I found myself studying each bottle, wondering if it smelled like summer or winter. I began to go through the motions of tasting at dinner, at parties, and while writing. And it dawned on me. I couldn't shoot live wine reviews every day, but I could certainly *write* them.

I started my blog *Wine. All the Time.* in 2012 and something just clicked. It was as if I had given myself permission to do what I had secretly, deep down wanted to do this whole time. To sit and be present with wine, to smell it and taste it, and to feel and just daydream. With each wine, I'd spend hours reading and researching, teaching myself about varietals and regions and winemaking, and writing my reviews, for no particular reason except that I enjoyed doing it. Virtually no one read it for years, but I didn't care. The blog was for me, for those few moments of peace, for that feeling of somewhere else.

In February 2015, I got an e-mail from *New York Magazine* for an interview with *Grub Street* about *Wine Time*. I was flattered and excited, but I didn't think much of it. By this point, I'd been working as Mindy Kaling's assistant for four years and had written enough scripts, taken enough meetings, and performed in enough UCB Theatre storytelling shows to never get my hopes up about anything. Not even like, "Oh, this could be great! Wait, better not get my hopes up." Just no hopes. Zero. Like it didn't even cross my mind that this interview about my wine writing and videos could be the thing that launched my dream career.

A week after the interview went up, I had a literary agent and started the proposal for this book. By June, I had quit my job, was writing for VICE's *Munchies*, won the Editors' Choice and the Readers' Choice for Best Wine Coverage at the *Saveur* Blog Awards, and sold this book. And that December, out of nowhere, my favorite magazine offered me a job as their wine columnist.

The moral of the story is, if I can go from chugging $2 Cabernet on the Internet to writing about wine professionally for *Bon Appétit*, then fuck yes, you can pick out notes of bell pepper in a Cabernet Franc. Especially because I'm not sending you off to start a blog and spend the next five years collecting an education by your lonesome. Nope, we're doing this together, you and me, homie. I'm going to guide you through fermentations and sparkling wine methods, teach you how to navigate wine labels and how to swirl without spilling on your new shoes, and even tell you some of my secrets, like how I buy wine, how I survive family functions, and how I stopped hating Chardonnay. It's everything you need to know to drink well, right now.

By the end of this book, you will be a confident wine drinker. You will know how wine is made, you will smell red fruits, you will be as comfortable talking tasting notes as you are parsing pop culture. You will enter wine shops with an assured air about you, you will take the wine list at restaurants without hesitation, you will volunteer to bring a bottle to pair with your mother-in-law's famous pasta. You won't get a lapel pin, nor will you know everything, but I don't either. And you don't need to to kick ass and drink good wine. Promise.

Disclaimer

Dear Reader,

This book is a lighthearted primer for the wine consumer who wishes to know more about wine but is not interested in discussing what pH level qualifies a wine as *flabby* (yet). If you happen to be a sommelier, or are taking sommelier courses, or just happened to watch the *Somm* movies and are a dick about it, you probably know most of what I'll cover in this book. While I believe this book will still be entertaining and valuable to you, I mention this because I don't need your Amazon reviews about how you already knew everything in this book. No shit! You're a sommelier, and genuinely, congratulations, because that is a huge accomplishment. But this isn't an advanced course on the Rheingau. I'm writing this book for me five years ago, who wished I had something to help get me started, and everyone else who has been wishing that they had this type of primer, too.

But for all interested parties, I hope you buy this book, read it, and find yourself enjoying wine more than ever before. No flash cards required.

Cheers,
Marissa A. Ross
Leisure Enthusiast, Author, & *Bon Appétit* Wine Columnist

Glossary

DEFINITIONS, KEY PHRASES, & WORDS
THAT MAY OR MAY NOT MATTER

Let me just say up front that I'm never going to tell you how to talk about wine. That'd be like walking up to some innocent onlooker at an art museum expressing their feelings about a particular painting and being like, "No, no. You actually must talk about your reaction to Basquiat *like this*!" It strips away everything organic, honest, and creative from the experience. But just like any other subject or industry, the wine world has a lot of terminology that normal-ass people have no use for in their everyday lives, but that you still need to be familiar with. While I one hundred percent encourage you to describe a glass of your favorite Zweigelt as "dope," slang isn't going to help you buy wine in stores, order it at restaurants, or find common ground with your fingers-crossed-future-father-in-law over dinner. We simply can't discuss wine with everyone without first learning the dialect.

We also can't protect ourselves without educating ourselves. First of all, there is a ton of misinformation out there in the world. People overhear some gossip at a dinner party and treat it as gospel because some dude named George spent

a weekend in Tuscany and therefore he must be a real author-
ity. Look, George doesn't know shit. But neither do most people, so they believe what they hear and repeat it to a bunch of
other people who also don't know shit who then believe it and
repeat it. Suddenly, everyone is going around claiming they
drink "sulfite-free" wine when that is a physical impossibil-
ity. And second, you can't spar with an asshole who uses wine
words as a weapon unless you know them, too. Cynical, I know.
I would love to be proven wrong, and genuinely hope you never
have to deal with this, but from my experience, you're going
to. People love being assholes about wine, and although you
should definitely just walk away from these interactions, it's
always nice to be able to throw your middle fingers in the air
while coming correct on some douche bag who thought they
could stump you with *phylloxera*.

Not today, snob.

Not today.

Normally, a glossary is in the back of the book, but for the
purpose of preparing you for the chapters ahead, I'm giving
it to you now. Take a little time to get acquainted with the
vocab to save yourself from constantly having to look shit up.

A

Acid/Acidity: Acid/acidity is the sour quality of a wine. It is
caused by acids in the grapes themselves and/or the fermentation process.

Aeration: You know how some people need time to open up?
So do some wines. Aeration is when you purposefully expose

wine to air to help it breathe and soften its acidity and tannins. Many winemakers aerate their wines during the winemaking process, but you can also aerate wine in a decanter or with one of those fancy aerating devices you got for Christmas. Or you can just pour it in a glass and let it chill out for a while, and boom, you just aerated that shit!

Aging: This is when you leave a bottle for a while and hope that when you come back to it, it has grown the fuck up and is finally ready for a real relationship. Just kidding . . . kinda. Aging is when you leave a bottle unopened for an extended period in hopes that it softens and becomes more complex as its components meld together over time. So yeah, it does grow up! To age wines, you need to store them somewhere with a cool temperature. Ideally, at cellar temperature, which is 54 degrees. Since most of us do not have a wine cellar, you can store them in a small wine fridge, in the darkest, coolest corner of your closet, or even under your bed if your room doesn't get too hot. Aging varies from wine to wine, so do some research. You don't need to be crafting vinegar under your mattress.

Alcohol: That thing we love! And hate! Produced during fermentation, alcohol is a chemical compound created when yeasts consume natural grape sugars, and in the infamous words of Dave Chappelle as Samuel L. Jackson, "It'll get you drunk!"

Alcohol by Volume: ABV is the measurement of how much alcohol is in a wine and one of the most important things to look at on a wine's label. The ABV in wine varies wildly, with wines as low as 9 percent alcohol to heavy reds that can get up around 15 percent. You want to pay attention to this, because pounding a bottle of 14.5 percent Petite Sirah can really fuck you up.

Appearance: What a wine looks like, particularly its color and clarity.

Appellation: A legally designated region where grapes are grown and wine is made, like Champagne or Napa. Some appellations have certain laws and rules that winemakers must abide by in order to use the appellation on the label of their wine. For example, wait for it . . .

Appellation d'Origine Contrôlée: Usually abbreviated to AOC, Appellation d'Origine Contrôlée is a designated and approved appellation in France that has certain regulations by which wines must be made. With rules for everything from what varietals can be grown, to how much can be grown, to which winemaking methods can be used, AOCs protect the geographical areas and ensure winemaking standards.

Aromatic: A nice way of saying that a wine has a strong smell, or has more smells going on than an eighth-grade boys' locker room.

Astringent: Descriptor for heavy or too much tannin. It's a sharp, sucking feeling that leaves your mouth drier than the time you smoked weed out of your sister's three-foot bong.

AVA: Stands for American Viticultural Area, which is basically America's version of the AOC without the rules. For example, Napa is an AVA. This means it is recognized as a region where grapes grow, but there are no regulations for growing the grapes or anything similar. They're just like, "This is a place with grapes. Cool."

B

Balance: When all of a wine's components—such as fruit, acid, tannin, and alcohol—work together and create a harmonious taste on your tongue. Nothing feels out of place.

Big: A descriptor used for wines with so much flavor that they feel like they're filling your entire mouth. And not just in an "Oh, wow, I just took a really big sip" way.

Bitter: Used to describe a wine with a sharp, well, bitter taste. It can be caused by unripe grapes, tannins, or just your personal palate.

Blend: The combination of several different grapes to create a wine. It can be for a specific blend, like a winery's "red field blend," or it can be used for creating balance or complexity in a seemingly single varietal wine. This is why you will see a bottle labeled Cabernet but on the back you will see it also is 10 percent Merlot. I know, it's confusing, because you're like, "Why is it called Cabernet, then, if it's not just Cabernet?!" Because they're allowed to, that's why.

Body: The weight of a wine in your mouth. Literally how heavy it feels when you drink it.

Botrytis Cinerea: Also known as the **noble rot**, *botrytis* is a good, gray mold that enhances a wine's flavor and sweetness by concentrating the grape's acids and sugars. This naturally occurring mold usually is found in cool, damp vineyards, and while winemakers may try to prevent it on certain grapes, they like it on sweeter wine grapes like Riesling and Tokaji.

Bottle Aged: When a wine has been aged for a substantial amount of time in the bottle. It's like aging, except this is usually done before the wine is available in retail.

Bouquet: The aromas of a wine, sometimes referred to as "the nose."

Brilliant: Classically, this means the wine is crystal clear, but I say you can use it for expressing that you think a wine is deliciously genius.

Brix: A unit of sugar used in the winemaking process to predict how much alcohol will be in a wine.

Brut: Pretty fucking dry Champagne, with less than 1.5 percent residual sugar.

BTB: An abbreviation meaning wine is served "by the bottle," usually used on hip restaurant lists to let you know they "get" young people.

BTG: An abbreviation meaning wine served "by the glass," because btw tbh TL;DR young people *love* abbreviations.

Bulk Wine: Any unbottled wine that is in mass quantity, usually sold to other companies to bottle and sell under their own label. As a consumer, you may not hear this often, but it is good to know because if you hear a wine is from bulk wine, then you know the winery whose label is on the bottle did not make the wine themselves.

Bung: A cork that is placed into the bunghole, a circular opening in a barrel of wine that is used for getting the wine in and out of the barrels during the winemaking process.

Buttery: Used to describe wine that smells or tastes like butter, usually caused by malolactic fermentation.

C

Cap: The mass of grape skins, stems, and seeds that forms at the top of the tank during a red wine's fermentation.

Carbon Dioxide: Gas created during fermentation; also what makes wine effervescent.

Carbonic Maceration: When full clusters of grapes are fermented whole, rather than being crushed before fermentation. Individual grapes go through fermentation as the grapes are crushed under their own weight. This is what makes Beaujolais and other red wines taste extra poppy.

Chaptalization: The addition of sugar during the fermentation process to increase alcohol levels. Considered shady and gross by many, especially those in the natural wine community.

Charmat Method: Also known as the Tank Method of sparkling wines, where the second fermentation to create bubbles is done in a big tank.

Chewy: Used to describe a full, textural wine that feels a little like you just mowed down a bag of gummy bears. Like you need to chew it.

Closed: Used to describe when a wine needs to breathe for a bit, or young wines that probably needed to be aged longer and now you're bummed that you got excited and opened it too early.

Cloudy: When a wine's appearance is foggy-looking. This is common for wines that have not been filtered or fined.

Coarse: Descriptor used when a wine's texture is literally scratchy, like you're licking sandpaper, usually because of a high concentration of tannins.

Cold Fermentation: When the fermentation vessel, usually steel tanks, is cooled, creating a slower fermentation that helps preserve a wine's aromas and flavors.

Complex: Used to describe a wine's flavor that changes as you drink it, or if there's a lot going on and you don't even know where to start.

Corked: When a wine has been tainted by the chemical trichloro-anisole (TCA). The wine, not the cork itself, will smell like wet dog or musty newspapers. This is also called cork taint.

Crush: The compressing of grapes before fermentation.

D

Decant: To let wine breathe and have it, hopefully, taste better in an hour.

Demi-Sec: French way of saying "moderately sweet."

Depth: The intensity of a wine's flavor.

Destemmer: A machine used to destem grapes before they're crushed.

Dirty: Some people use this as a negative term to describe faulty, poorly made wine. I use it to describe textural, natural wines that taste dirty, as in literal dirt. Usually in a positive manner. Unless I'm saying, "This tastes like dirt." But even then, that can be a good thing!

Disgorging: The process in which the lees, the sediment from yeast and other particles, are removed from sparkling wines after second fermentation.

Dry: Used to describe wines that have very little residual sugar (less than 0.2 grams), and taste literally dry. Can be used to describe tannins as well, although make sure to clarify that in mixed company.

E

Earthy: Descriptor for when a wine tastes like anything relating to the earth itself, like soil, dust, plants, or even some vegetables such as mushrooms. If it tastes like you've picked it off the ground, it's earthy.

Elegant: Used to describe graceful, smooth wines. Jackie Kennedy vibes, not "Mom dancing to a Jimmy Buffett cover band after too many margaritas" vibes.

Enology: The science and study of winemaking, not to be confused with viticulture (the study of grape growing) but fine to be confused with oenology because it's the same thing.

Estate Bottled: Bottled on site of the vineyard, as opposed to wines that are bottled at an outside facility.

Esters: Aromatic compounds created during fermentation by yeasts and bacteria. Esters are the reason why, as you're swirling and smelling your wine, you detect the scent of anything but grapes.

Extra Dry: Extra dry has 1.2–2.0 grams of residual sugar, making it sweeter than "dry" and totally ass-backward. I don't get it either.

F

Fat: Another way to say "full-bodied," although I think it's a little rude.

Fermentation: Wine's naturally occurring game of Pac-Man, where the yeast eats the sugar and converts it to alcohol and carbon dioxide. Thus making WINE!

Filtering: The process of removing sediment from a wine.

Fining: When they add clarifying agents (aka gross additives) to make a wine's appearance clearer.

Finish: That lasting sensation a wine leaves in your mouth after you've swallowed it.

Flat: When a wine tastes dull and boring, most likely because it doesn't have enough acidity.

Flowery: When a wine smells or tastes like you shoved a bouquet of flowers in your face. (Or even just a couple of flowers.)

Fortified: When a wine has the addition of wine spirits added, such as port, sherry, and vermouth.

Free Run: Juice that is produced under the weight of the grapes after harvest. That juice is freeeeeeee, freeeeeee runnin'. Wines can be made entirely of this free run juice, or it is added to the pressed juice.

Fruity: Adjective used to describe wines that smell heavily of fruit, whether it be jammy dark berry fruits in red wines or bright citrus or tropical fruits in white wines.

Full-Bodied: A wine that is heavy, leaving a weighty feeling in your mouth.

G

Glou-Glou: French slang for wines that you can drink like water, and glug glug glug down the gullet.

Grassy: A descriptor used for wines that smell or taste like grass, like actual grass, not the Cheech & Chong grass. Most commonly found in white wines like Sauvignon Blanc, grassiness is caused by compounds in the wine that also happen to be found in actual grass.

Green: Used to describe wines that have a plant or vegetable vibe to their aroma and/or flavor.

H

Herbaceous: When a wine smells and/or tastes like garden herbs. Not the kind you smoke. Okay, *maybe*.

Hot: An out-of-whack wine with way too much alcohol.

I

Isinglass: Fining agent made from fish bladders; used for clarifying wine during winemaking. Ick.

J

Jammy: When a wine tastes like thick, rich berry jam.

L

Lees: Yeast cells and other particles that have settled after fermentation.

Legs: The streaks or tears on the side of a wineglass that some people will try to tell you is indicative of a wine's quality. It's not. The bigger the streaks, the more alcohol in the wine. Considering the ABV is listed on the bottle, there's no need to inspect legs like they're the key to a good glass.

Light-Bodied: When a wine is thin, and literally light, in your mouth.

Malolactic Fermentation: Process that chemically converts sharp, strong acid into softer lactic acid and is what creates that "buttery" flavor in wines like Chardonnay.

Mouthfeel: The texture of a wine and, truly, how it feels in your mouth. Examples are silky, juicy, rough, or like running your tongue along an unpaved road.

Must: The juice and pulp of skins, seeds, and stems created after you've crushed the grapes.

Musty: A dirty, humid attic smell that is not good in attics or in wine.

New World: Wines from countries that started producing wines after the fifteenth century; basically after France, Italy, Germany, and other European countries got into the wine-making game.

Nonvintage: A Champagne term for when several batches of wine from many different years are blended together. This is how most Champagne is made, so nothing to judge about.

Nose: How a wine smells; same thing as *bouquet*.

O

Oaky: The flavor that oak fermentation leaves in a wine. Sometimes it's faint and sometimes it can be very strong. Different oaks for different folks!

Oenology: The science and study of winemaking (also *enology*). When you see people tacking *oeno* onto words, this is why.

Off-Dry: Just a little sweet, like a smidge (but if you're sensitive to sweet wines, it's probably still too sweet).

Old World: Countries that have been making wine SINCE THE BEGINNING OF TIME. Well, the beginning of time for wine, that is, since Old World countries such as France, Italy, Spain, Germany, Portugal, and Greece are where winemaking originated.

Oxidation: When a wine is exposed to oxygen. This can happen during fermentation, on purpose, to create a maple-y flavor in a wine, but it can also happen after the wine has already been bottled, which ruins the wine and is considered a fault.

P

Phylloxera: The Black Plague of grapevines. Phylloxera is an aphid—you know, those teeny tiny black bugs you've probably seen in the garden, hanging on roses and shit?—that attacks grapevine roots, absorbing its water and nutrients, until the vine dies. It has wiped out millions of acres of grapevines, and the only known solution is to rip up the vines, replant the vineyard with Native American rootstocks that are tolerant of phylloxera, and then graft another grapevine onto the new vine.

Press: To take destemmed and crushed grapes and squeeze out any remaining juice.

Private Reserve: Sometimes this term is for legit private releases sold only at a winery or to a winery's club members,
and other times it's something a winery throws on the label
to make people think it's a legit special release. It's an unregulated term, so use your best judgment.

Producer: A winemaker that is also involved with growing
the grapes.

Pulp: The fleshy inside of a grape.

Pump-Over: When a hose is used to pull wine out from the
bottom of a fermentation tank and pour it back over the top
to mix the juice with its skins.

Punch-Down: When the skins of grapes have risen to the top
of the fermentation tank, they are pushed down manually to
mix the juice with its skins.

R

Racking: During barrel fermentation, sediment settles at the
bottom of the barrel. The free juice is then syphoned from its
barrel into a clean, sediment-free barrel.

Reserve Wine: This is supposed to be a higher-quality release
from wineries, but the terminology isn't regulated, so it can
be slapped on anything. Except wines from Washington
State. Washington has it regulated so that only wines that

are 10 percent or less of a winemaker's production and are the highest-priced wines may use the term *reserve*.

Residual Sugar: Natural sugars left behind after fermentation that weren't converted to alcohol. You may hear it also referred to as RS. While this does make a wine sweeter, it doesn't give off a gross saccharine-sweet taste like added sugar.

Riddling (*Remuage*): Where sparkling wines are placed with their necks tilted downward and are regularly rotated to collect the lees in the neck before disgorgement.

S

Secondary Fermentation: There are two types of secondary fermentations. There's the good type, where wines purposefully go through a second fermentation to become sparkling wines (huzzah)! And then there is the bad type, where a nonsparkling wine goes through a second fermentation in the bottle but you don't know until you open it up and it's awful. It will be a bit bubbly, and it will taste like a hamster's cage.

Sediment: All the leftover goodies from winemaking, like yeasts, grape skins, and seeds.

Sentiment: The word my computer always corrects *sediment* to because it knows I am an emotional creature.

Settling: What you're doing in that relationship right now. Just kidding! It's when you open up a wine that has been aging and there's sediment in the bottle from molecules and tannins bonding over the years.

Skin Contact: Even though all red wines ferment with their skins, the term *skin contact* refers to white wines that are crushed with their skins and left hanging together for anywhere from a few hours to days, depending on the flavor the winemaker wishes to achieve.

Smoky: When a wine smells or tastes like someone just fired up the grill or a cigar.

Sommelier: A trained and certified wine professional, specializing in wine related to fine dining.

Sour: Used to describe a wine with sharp acidity. Some people see this as a bad thing, but as a kid who used to eat packs of Warheads like they were fruit snacks, I use it liberally and positively.

Spicy: A wine that smells and/or tastes like it's been hanging out with your spice rack.

Spritzy: Slight effervescence. Can be good in wines that are supposed to have a little bubble, but not great if it's a table wine. May mean it has had a second fermentation in bottle.

Stemmy: Used to describe wines that smell and/or taste like green plant stems. If it has an astringency to it, *stemmy* may refer to the grape stems themselves.

Sulfur: A naturally occurring chemical in wine, produced from fermentation. Naturally occurring sulfur is a preservative and antimicrobial agent that is actually very helpful to wine. Added sulfur is also commonly used to maintain a wine's freshness and protect it from oxidation so it can age for long periods of time.

T

Terroir: Looks like a terror to pronounce (it's *tare-wah*, by the way), but it's the French word for the entire environment where a wine is produced, including the soil, climate, and surrounding vegetation.

V

Varietal: A specific type of grape.

Vintner: Old-school term for winemaker.

Vintage: The specific year the grapes were harvested to make a wine.

Vitis Vinifera: Grape varietal native to Europe.

W

Winemaker: Someone who is in charge of the winemaking process but doesn't necessarily grow the grapes. A winemaker can do both, but wineries can hire winemakers to come in to make wines out of grapes they grow on their own.

Obviously, this glossary doesn't contain all the words that exist in the world of wine, but it's enough to get you started and, most important, to keep you from getting totally confused as we venture forth and begin your foray into drinking wine like a badass who knows what the fuck is up. Or at the very least, knows how to taste, buy, and enjoy wine more than you did before.

CHAPTER ONE

If I Can Go from Two Buck Chuck to Connoisseur, So Can You

I wasn't kidding when I said I started where you are right now. Maybe even further behind where you are right now. I was a broke writer who drank absolute shit wines up until maybe five years ago, and then I was still a broke writer because I was spending all my money on wine. But all those years, from the worst wines of twenty-two to the best wines of thirty, have been my education. In this chapter, we'll go over the bottles I drank in the beginning, the lessons they taught me, and my philosophies in tasting that I still use to this day.

MY JOURNEY IN WINE, FROM FRANZIA TO CAB FRANC

Most people think learning about wine is a strenuous and academic endeavor reserved for aspiring sommeliers. While that is one way to do it, it isn't the only way. My preferred method is much simpler: Drink a lot of wine, and be conscious of what you're drinking. In other words, with each wine you drink, you should be taking mental or physical notes on it, and reading up on any grape, producer, region, or even just words on the label you're not familiar with. It's important to do this while you're drinking the wine (granted you're not at the dinner table and being rude as hell) so that the information you're recording or researching sticks with your memory of the wine itself. And that's it: a crash course in the Marissa A. Ross School of Wine. I've never taken any classes, nor did I turn twenty-one and, poof, became a wine connoisseur. Everything I know today comes from years of drinking progressively less shitty wine.

It all started with Franzia White Zinfandel. Franzia White Zinfandel smells like moldy oranges covered in corn syrup and tastes like a melted pack of knockoff Sour Patch Kids you found between car seats. As much as I want to fondly remember it as the wine my grandmother drank with ice cubes, instead it ignites nightmarish memories of a cheerleader making me chug twelve ounces of it spiked with gin. I know technically you can't spike something that is already alcoholic, but if someone puts gin in your Zin, trust me, it's spiked. Hell, it's practically roofied. Since that fateful evening my sophomore year of high school, I have not touched Franzia nor trusted anyone named Erika.

That first taste of alcohol didn't turn me off from wine as a whole. In college, I took to Quail Oak Cabernet. It really captures that whole *"I'm going to college! Just kidding, I'm skipping class to smoke weed because I have no idea what the hell I'm doing"* vibe with its scent of a week-old open can of plums in a dirty dorm room and long finish of cheap, hot alcohol left out in the yard after a frat party. Miraculously, seventy cents less than Charles Shaw, Quail Oak pairs with your roommate's leftover pizza and getting drunk enough to watch a movie (read: do hand stuff) with a relative stranger you met in the political science class you went to twice last semester. Born out of necessity and seeped in shame, it is the wine equivalent of smoking a resin bowl, something I became all too familiar with after I dropped out of college and moved back home my sophomore year.

When I moved to Los Angeles in 2008, I had a big dream of becoming a comedy writer/actor, three soul-crushing day jobs later—and two Craigslist roommates, one of whom turned out to be a Craigslist drug dealer, while the other was a heroin addict, hoarder, Craigslist hooker—I took to writing (hiding) in my closet-size room with my $3 wines. They were all I could afford, and I liked them enough, but it just made me think if I liked $3 wines, I'd probably *love* $5 wines. Despite not having the money for such indulgences, I took the leap and started buying $5 Rex-Goliath Pinot Noir. You wouldn't believe how much of a difference two dollars make. Instead of smelling like rotting fruit, the Rex-Goliath smelled like my old aunt's perfume. Instead of tasting like I was about to have regrettable sex with a clumsy coed, it tasted like I was about to have regrettable sex with a selfish photographer/barista. Most important, it had a different texture than the $3 wines I'd been drinking. I don't know if I would go as far as to call it "lush & velvety!" like their little gold stickers do, but there was a weight to it, with two actual notes of fruit and spice, rather than one note of booze.

Society had made it clear that I was not a woman until I started drinking white wine, and so at age twenty-four, I stepped into adulthood. I had hated white wine until I tried the Beringer Sauvignon Blanc. A serious splurge at $6, Beringer smelled musty, like the boxes of yearbooks my mom made me move out of her garage and I was like, "Mom! Just because I'm a woman doesn't mean I have a place for my old yearbooks! You have a garage! I have a shoe box in the city! I don't have room for these! FINE, I'LL TAKE THEM! I'M A GROWN WOMAN! I DRINK SAUVIGNON BLANC." It tasted like a recently cleaned litter box mixed with citrus rinds, and felt like a cool breeze blowing through my hair, as if I was in a convertible speeding down the highway of maturity, Chuck Shaw in my rearview mirror. Suddenly, I was ordering salmon at restaurants and watching *Top Chef*, because that is adult shit.

It was around this time that I started making friends who were a little older and more successful than I. They would throw dinner parties, *real* dinner parties, not like the veggie corn dogs and bricks of cheddar cheese dinner parties I'd throw for myself and my Netflix queue. Going to these events, I knew I couldn't show up with a $2 or even $6 bottle of wine. I had to step up my game, so I started buying $12 Coppola wine *on sale*. Coppola wine smelled like, "Are you sure you wanted to spend $12 on this? Cause you broke, girl, and this is like four bottles' worth of money." But then you taste it and you're like, wait, there are wines that are smooth? It was fruity but soft, and that was the first time I thought a wine felt "plush." I'd heard people use the word *plush* before, but it hadn't ever clicked before this. It tasted like, "I'm not drinking this to just get drunk. I'm drinking it because I like it! And because I can't embarrass myself in front of a bunch of thirty-year-olds with real jobs." I still embarrassed myself, but I took comfort in the fact that no one could say I went on Louis C.K.–style rants *and* brought $2 wine.

At this point, I had developed a small cult following for my personal blog, where I documented all my cheap wine drinking. I felt safe embracing and making fun of myself online as a broke writer and shit wine drinker, but secretly, deep down, I wanted to feel more confident about my abilities to taste and understand wine. I knew that going to a wine tasting could open up those doors for me, but I was nervous about it. Going to a tasting was terrifying because it was going to be real wine, from a wine shop, not the cheap, sugary stuff I drank all the time. I couldn't hide behind jokes or my computer screen, and I felt very vulnerable. But for $15, I could get three glasses of wine, and in Los Angeles, that's the best deal in town. So I mustered up the courage to go to my local shop, Silverlake Wine, eager to learn but still feeling nervous. When I arrived, though, I didn't have time to be embarrassed, because as soon as I had my first flight, I was overcome with joy. I had never experienced so many different sensations in a single glass of wine, let alone three. I was too busy writing notes and savoring each sip to care about anything else, especially what other people thought of me.

Suddenly, wines didn't just taste like "wine." There were specific and singular notes working in harmony to create a beautiful song of flavor. Fruits and spices danced on my mid-palate, a part of my tongue I didn't even know could taste things on its own. I was enlightened and enamored; these tastings changed my life forever. I became obsessed with how wines differed from one another, how they each had their own flavor progression and their own sensations. I couldn't go back to drinking the same $6 wine every night—no, now I had to try *everything*.

This desire to try all new wines all the time pushed me to venture into unfamiliar varietals outside of California, which was a big deal for me. Although I was never allowed to drink as a youngster, I grew up in Southern California in the nineties, so wine was a huge part of my life. My father, a mortgage broker, and my mother, a country club housewife and class mom with a heart of gold, were very into entertaining. As a child, I remember sitting at dinner parties and listening to my parents and their guests go on and on about what they had tasted in Santa Barbara the past weekend or what Napa wine club they had just joined. I remember knowing that white wine wasn't "white wine," it was Chardonnay, and my father always served it with fish. And red wine wasn't "red wine," it was Cabernet and it was served with everything else. To me, these California wines were the epitome of being a successful adult.

Subsequently, I spent my early wine days drinking (cheap) California wines. At first, buying new wines felt like gambling in a foreign language—expensive and unfamiliar. Wagering $17 on a bottle of wine whose label is written in what looks like straight-up gibberish was a risky bet. What if I didn't like it? Then I've just thrown away $17 I could have spent on low-risk high-return items, such as dryer sheets and dog food.

But trying new wines had already become an addiction. Not only was I going to tastings regularly, I had started to take deep pleasure in writing about wines. I would open a bottle after work and sit alone with it, sipping it, letting it speak to me, and researching each different type of grape, otherwise known as a "varietal." I got bored drinking the same things, now for reasons even beyond my taste buds. I wanted to learn more, and I knew that drinking the same shit every week wasn't going to cut it.

I never had much of a strategy when buying wine; I'd look at the labels and pick out ones that were pretty, or came from a varietal I for sure already liked. This was not a very accurate way of doing things, so eventually, I decided to reduce my risk by calculating odds with the professionals, and always asking for their help. Without knowing it, this was one of the smartest moves I've ever made. By talking to the people who knew more about wine than I did, I was able to explore regions across the world, multitudes of varietals, and a wide array of winemaking styles with my trusted wine merchants as my guides. The more wines I tried, the less of a gamble it became. Instead, each new bottle became an opportunity to learn about wine, the world, and myself. I realized that wine was not a gamble at all, but an experience. It's abstract yet personal, allowing you to indulge in the moment of how it physically tastes while also evoking memories from taste and sensations past. In wine, there are no rules. A bottle of wine can remind you of your adolescent summers at the beach and a field in France you've never seen, in the same sip.

And this is why you know more about wine than you give yourself credit for. You've dreamed of distant lands, you know the smell of an old leather purse, and you've tasted fresh fruit. Maybe a bunch of cheerleaders didn't take advantage of you as a dorky sixteen-year-old theater kid and throw a party at your house while your parents were out of town and get you grounded for three fucking months, but I'm sure you have your own reasons for wanting to step up your game beyond cheap boxed wine. Drawing upon your memory and your senses is the foundation of tasting, enjoying, and learning about wine.

Wine is an acquired knowledge. Each glass is a lesson, whether it comes from a bottle from a gas station or a fancy cellar. No matter what you're drinking, you're learning. All it takes is you wanting it—and considering you're here, I know you do.

APPROACH WINE LIKE YOU DO SMALL PLATES

A lot of people are crazy about food. I get it. Food is delicious! But it's wild how you can take totally normal humans, place a menu in front of them, and suddenly they transform into some sort of culinary Evel Knievels, willing to try anything. Rather than jumping over semitrucks, they're ordering five to ten small plates of shit you've never heard of. Beef heart tartare? Fried quail eggs? Some sort of molecular papaya yogurt dessert that looks like well-plated jizz? SURE! WHY NOT!

There's something about food culture that makes people feel like they should go outside of their comfort zones. I have friends who need to eat the spiciest thing at the spiciest Thai restaurant in town, the meal ending with us sweating and snotting with swollen, crying eyes. People wait in line for hours when a fabled burger joint opens in their neighborhood. And when society decided to start interbreeding baked goods, no one would shut up about it. People want the trendiest, weirdest, craziest, tastiest shit all the time. They eat it up! (bah-dum-chhhhh)

I'm not above this behavior (aside from cross-pollinated pastries, which I have zero interest in) and I actively participate in it. I love new restaurants, experimental dishes, and innovative chefs. I plan meals around Jonathan Gold reviews, spend free time caressing last month's *Bon Appétit*, and consider Anthony Bourdain a god. I *get* the food thing. What I don't get is how people are so reluctant to take that same curiosity and fervent thrill-seeking attitude they have with food and apply it to how they approach wine. How is it so easy for some to order something like veal brains but dither over wine lists, only to order the one Pinot Noir they recognize?

Our whole lives, we're encouraged to try new foods. As children, the most mundane and normal-ass foods are totally bonkers to us. Parents have to constantly urge their kids to try something as simple and universally delicious as mashed potatoes because hello, they're trying to keep you alive. As adults, these persuasions come from our social life. How many times have you been out to dinner and your date is like, "C'mon! Just try it! It's so good!" And you probably did, depending on how much you love food and/or wanted to get laid. This process is how we find out what we like and also, just as important, what we don't like.

Here's an example: I once tried bone marrow when out with a group of friends for my husband's birthday at a restaurant called Bestia. I'm a big texture person, so someone describing something as "meat jelly" made me want to just throw up and die right there. But my feeling was "Well, if I'm ever going to try bone marrow, this is the place to do it." Did I like it? Fuck no, I didn't like it! It's fucking meat jelly! Out of a bone! It's like something out of a Martha Stewart Halloween spread next to the peeled grape eyeballs! Except real! And disgusting! But still, I tried it. It didn't go to waste with the bunch of food-loving monsters I hang around with, but even if all of us tried it and didn't like it, we would have just left the half-eaten bone on the table and not thought twice about it.

There is no inherent habit to try new things when it comes to wine because "trying new things" with alcohol has been historically disastrous for most of us. "Trying new things" is what led you to "trying" about thirty-five whipped cream–topped shots called Scooby Snacks, streaking through a house party, and jumping off the diving board like a goddamn Will Ferrell character. No, thanks, "trying new things." We want what we know we like and what we know will not turn us into animals. Anything outside of those parameters is asking for trouble. Can't risk it!

There is something so precious about wine that not liking a wine or, heaven forbid, not finishing a bottle is seen as a blasphemous waste. Trying a new dish is fun and fleeting, but buying a bottle of wine is a commitment that can last the whole meal. It feels more justifiable to put your money on something reliable than on the unknown. But that unknown is so important! That unknown is your first time visiting a foreign country. That unknown is the first time you had sex, or went to a concert, or read the book that changed your worldview. The unknown is everything you've ever been excited about, food or otherwise. To actively avoid the unknown in wine is to actively avoid a source of pleasure and inspiration.

I know it's easier to throw money at $10 tapas than $70 bottles of wine, and I'm not saying you should just go to restaurants and randomly pick the wackiest shit off the wine list. But what I am saying is that you should take that daring spirit that drives you to try a wild dish or cook a new recipe, and try a bottle of wine you've never had before. Life is too short not to venture past Pinot Noir.

WINE IS NOT MATH

The only thing in this world that rivals my passion toward wine is my passionate hatred of math. I was one of those kids that scored a seven-hundred-and-something on my SATs, and that score came entirely from the English portion. I would've had a better chance of performing decently on the

math section had I just gone ahead and drawn a huge anar-
chist circle-A through the answer sheet, or perhaps just set it
on fire.

My problem with math was that I never wanted to accept
that there was only one right answer. I realize that math is
this way for legitimate reasons, like logic and science and to
torture children, and I respect that. But to this day, I'm still
like, "Fuck that shit."*

This is why it pains me to see new wine drinkers treat
wine like it's an equation to be solved out of a textbook.
Sometimes when you ask someone what they think about the
wine, they clam up as if they've been called to the chalkboard
to answer a question off the homework they didn't complete.
You can see their mind racing. The correct fruit descriptor
plus the correct body descriptor plus two words I don't quite
understand but have heard people use equals the correct as-
sessment of this wine. Marissa, did I get an A?

No, you didn't, because wine is not math. There is no
"right" or "wrong" answer, and objectivity in wine is a joke.
And that's not just my subjective opinion. The way a wine
tastes to you is influenced primarily by what you bring to it.
You have a myriad of expectations, prejudices, and precon-
ceived notions that no one else has that affects everything
you taste.

Many biases are derived from your personal experiences.
In my family, Cabernet Sauvignon was a revered staple,
something that was on the table every night and was enjoyed
immensely. It was also something that was bragged about

---

* I have not done math since 2005, and I feel great about it.

between my father and his business-suited dinner guests, and therefore I came to associate Cabernets with being success-ful, grown-up, and luxurious. So when I turned twenty-one, I started drinking Cabernet Sauvignon with dinner every night because it made me feel mature and successful. It re-minded me of a time before the mortgage industry crisis, when my family could afford the finer things in life. I loved it. But I can't tell you how much of me loving Charles Shaw Cab-ernet was because I actually liked how it tasted, or because it was familiar and represented a sense of affluence at a price I could afford.

On the other hand, I couldn't drink anything blush col-ored for years (remember, the cheerleaders). Just the sight of a rosé would bring up an involuntary gag. Now I love rosés! But there were a good eight years when I looked at them as if they were a serial killer I had barely escaped the grips of in an episode of *Law & Order: SVU.* You know the look. Like I ran into them on the subway and was like, "No . . . NOOOOO!" and then ran in the opposite direction into Olivia Benson's arms and she just happened to have a glass of Cab waiting for me because she is an angel.

You also can't discount cultural conditioning. The types of cuisines you grew up eating influence your taste buds and their thresholds for certain flavors. If you grew up eating sweeter flavors, you are likely to have an aversion to acidic wines, or if you're like me and can't get enough salt, you'd prefer a glass of water over a sweet glass of Riesling. Genetics can also play a role in your taste. Some people have a bitter receptor gene called TAS2R38, or as we're going to call it, "that bitter receptor." If you have it, you are much more

sensitive to bitter flavors. Not only will you shy away from radicchio and grapefruit, but you'll also be averse to red wines
with heavy tannins, that astringent sensation that feels like
cotton mouth.

The expectation that we will all hit the same checklist of
descriptors in a wine is unrealistic. There are too many biases
that cannot be eliminated. What am I going to do? *Eternal
Sunshine* that semester you spent in Prague out of you? No.
That's totally impractical and inhumane since you probably
had a great time and why would I take that from you, even if
it means you hate my favorite Spanish biodynamic Carignan
because of some weirdo you had a one-night stand with? I
want your opinion, whether it is based on your knowledge and
appreciation of varietals, or it's based on your knowledge
and appreciation of life.

There is a good chance you're going to come across some
wines you just don't like, with or without bitter receptors. I've
come around on all sorts of things I never thought I would
come around on: Chardonnay, Merlot, Brussels sprouts, Birken-
stocks. But then, there are some tastes you just can't shake.
I've spent most of my wine career avoiding Moscato. A favorite of sorority sisters and hip-hop stars, Moscato is a wine
made all over the world, from California to Brazil to Italy. It
is fruity frizzante that is low in alcohol and made from Muscat Blanc grapes. They have a distinct aroma that is musky
with floral perfumes and some grapefruit, and while they *al-
legedly* taste like peaches with a medium body, to me it tastes
like a cup of fruit cocktail from elementary school that has
been left open in your fridge for four months.

And it's fine that I don't like Moscato, because we're all

entitled to not like things.* There will be plenty of people you'll encounter over the course of your life who will tell you that you *need* to like something. They're going to shove glasses at you, begging you to give it the same glowing review that they did, because it validates them. And it's very easy to smile and nod your head and say that something is lovely, when you really want to tell them that it tastes like you just swallowed a soggy dryer sheet lubed up with melted Mike and Ikes. But you know what? You don't need to validate shit. **You're allowed to not like things.** Don't drink something just because you feel obligated to.

It's not worth drinking wine with someone who is waiting for you to fawn or fuck up. There isn't a game show host holding his breath on your descriptors like, "Oooh, sorry, Tamara, it was not 'jammy.' The word we were looking for was 'fleshy.' *'Fleshy.'* But we have some lovely parting gifts for you!" And if anyone makes you feel that way, they are a huge asshole and you should take the parting gifts and run.

So drink and say whatever you want. It's a free and clear expression of your spirit. If a Sauvignon Blanc tastes like bobsledding down a field of wildflowers, then that is what it tastes like. I've never bobsledded, but I know exactly what bobsledding down a field of wildflowers tastes like, because I've drank enough Marlborough Sauvignon Blanc and that's what I decided it tastes like. Because wine is not math. Wine is a creative writing course. And this is me giving you poetic license to drink and describe wine however you'd like to.

---

* It would be irresponsible of me not to tell you that as of fall 2016, I have finally found a bottle of Moscato I love. This is a reminder to us all to try everything, but still, if you don't like something, you don't have to drink it. That's why there are dump buckets. Or you find a planter.

GIVING A SHIT ABOUT WINE DOESN'T MAKE YOU A SNOB

I've been called a "wine snob" a fair amount of times. Perhaps I deserved it once or twice (I have been known to get drunk and sassy, so it's definitely in the realm of possibility), but usually I'm not doing anything to justify that label. More often than not, I'm just giving a casual opinion, saying something like "I love the finish on this Trousseau!" when the eyes start rolling back into heads forever, never to be seen again.

Here's the thing: Drinking wine is just like anything else in the sense that if you spend enough time doing it, you're going to get good at it. The more wine you drink, the more refined your palate becomes. And I'm not saying "refined" like, *"Oh, you're an elegant person now,"* I'm saying "refined" as in you're going to be able to taste the difference between the bell peppers in a Cabernet Franc and the tobacco in Cabernet Sauvignon. Because you give a shit! And when you give a shit about wine, you're not just chugging it back without a thought. You are present with it. You start taking mental notes of varietals and region, and maybe real notes if you truly love it. And even if you have no idea what a wine is or where it is from, you are still smelling it and tasting it and thinking about it in a way that will help you become a more educated drinker. You may not remember it all overnight, but as you notice similar qualities reoccurring in what you drink, they become easier to recognize. And with that type of burgeoning knowledge base, of course you're going to have opinions! You're going to know what you like, what you don't, and most important, you're going to be able to articulate *why*. It starts small ("I like light-bodied reds"), but the next thing you know, you'll be talking about notes of blueberry pie and how you prefer stainless steel fermentation for Chardonnay.

This is seriously how every single hobby in the world works. You practice and you get better. The only difference is no one is going to call you a snob for taking up painting or joining an adult softball league.

And it will happen eventually. One day, it's going to hit you that the cheap wine you've been drinking all these years tastes awful and you'll swear off it, and someone is going to call you a snob. It has nothing to do with you being like, "Oooh, sorryyy. I'm too good for this." I mean, you'll drink it if you have to. You're not going to turn down shitty wine at your friend's art show if the only options are shitty wine or having to look at shitty paintings sober. But you're not bringing it home or taking it to a dinner party. Instead, you're going to take a wine you care about and start saying things like "Try the white cheddar with that Charbono I brought, Sharon! It's heavenly!" because you mean it. You're truly like, "Holy shit, white cheddar and Charbono are so good, how is everyone not freaking out about how good these two things taste together?!" And then some asshole you know across the snack spread is going to be like, "When did you become such a snob?" And then you grab the knife from the chèvre and stab them.

Because here's the thing: Giving a shit about wine doesn't make you a snob, it makes you an informed drinker.* And

---

* I now realize this sounds kinda snobby, so maybe don't go around calling yourself that, but between us it's cool.

being an informed wine drinker is the best kind of wine drinker because you're not going to be blindly drinking whatever has the coolest label. No more wandering aimlessly around the wine aisle, wondering what the hell any of it means. No more picking wine off the list just because it's not that cheap but also not that expensive. No more blowing money on wine you're not even sure you're going to like and then definitely not liking it and letting it turn into vinegar on your counter. Instead, you'll be recognizing varietals and regions, communicating what you're looking for, and making smarter purchases that lead to more enjoyable wine experiences.

When someone calls you a wine snob, they are actually telling you that they have been burned. At some point, someone belittled them over a beverage, and they feel the need to protect themselves from further judgment. I don't blame them for being defensive; you wouldn't want to be made to feel like a second-class citizen for not knowing how a specific cucumber was grown. But you can't take it personally.

How to Cure Yourself of Accidental Snobbery

But what if you realize [GASP] you *have* been getting a little snobby about your taste? Listen, it happens to the best of us. I was a snob once. Not a wine snob, but a Beatles snob. I spent about ten years of my life obsessing over the Beatles. I had all their records, read all their biographies, highlighted and memorized every important and totally unimportant date relevant to their careers. At any given moment, I was likely to tell you about what John Lennon was doing on this day in 1964. It was my "thing," and a very annoying one for anybody who was unlucky enough to be around me. I was convinced I loved the Beatles more than anyone, and I had to prove it.

The first time I did acid I was twenty, and John Lennon came to me. I mean, he didn't actually physically appear, but *ya know*. He told me I was an "unoriginal asshole" who was living my life by his words rather than my own and the Beatles were not a weapon for my pride. And that's pretty intense, for your god to basically come to you and tell you you're a shithead. But it was true. I knew it, and I threw out all my handmade flash cards the next day, never to look at another Beatles fact again.

The point is, if you're being a snob about wine, cut that shit out. It's gross and no one likes it. Don't wait until you do acid and have John Lennon come and tell you about it, because it will ruin your fucking life.

Snobs have dominated wine, the perception of it, and the conversation around it for far too long. We have to change that. Yes, you and me. I'm sorry to be putting you on the spot like this, but now that you're this far into the book, you're in

it with me. Don't worry—we're not throwing rallies or anything; it's a very low-commitment cause. Here is my foolproof
plan for ending wine snobbery for good:

1. Drink wine.
2. Share wine and wine knowledge freely and happily.
3. Encourage conversation.
4. DON'T BE A DICK.
5. Drink more wine.

And then people are like, "Wow, [insert your name here]
knows so much about wine! It's so cool! Plus, they're so at-
tractive and so funny and a really great host! I need to go out
and get that wine we had!" Then, because you treated them
like a human, they will do the same when they share that
wine with their friends. They will talk and laugh and learn
new things without the fear of judgment attached to it. It's a
chain reaction, baby. And it starts with us right now.

See, you and I aren't all that different! All of us have gotten
burned by boxed wine *at least* once, and it's totally okay that
you don't like Merlot. No matter what you're drinking, you're
learning, and are well on your way to becoming a confident
wine drinker. All you have to do is believe in yourself and believe in the process. It doesn't happen overnight; it takes time
and practice, so be patient with yourself. Give yourself permission to learn, to be open to knowledge wherever you find
it, and to be "right" or "wrong" and not care either way.

Because being a confident wine drinker isn't about knowing everything, it's about knowing there's always something to learn and being excited to drink it up.

~~To-Do~~ To-Drink List:

1. Treat yourself to a bottle of wine you've never heard of.
2. Talk or write about it freely without worrying about being "right."
3. Fuck math forever.

CHAPTER TWO

How Wine Is Made

Making wine is easy, right? You pick the grapes, smash 'em up, put 'em in a bottle, and voilà, wine! Wrong. Sorry, babe, but if it were that simple, I'd be using my juicer for a lot more than making empty promises about starting that detox cleanse. The winemaking process is a complicated one that varies from wine to wine and winemaker to winemaker, but having a general idea of what goes into making what's behind the label will give you not only a greater understanding of wine but a greater appreciation for it and the hardworking people who make it. In this chapter, I'm going to walk you through the process of winemaking, and by the end of it, you'll never call wine "adult juice" ever again.

We've all eaten grapes, and I would go as far as to say we've all drank grape juice, and probably even had our fair share of grape-flavored Popsicles (when there were no cherry ones left, of course). Yet, none of those things resemble wine and its complexities of flavors. Because while grapes are the star ingredient in wine, there is an incredible amount of technique, skill, and equipment that goes into making each bottle.

The first steps of winemaking are the same regardless of what kind of wine you're making.

First, you have to pick the grapes. Pretty straightforward, right? There are two methods for how this is done: mechanically or by hand.

With mechanical picking, winemakers use a tractor-looking machine to pick the grapes. And by "pick," I mean beat the vines to shake the fruit onto a conveyor belt that puts the grapes in a holding bin. This is more efficient for mass production because it cuts down on labor costs and picks a ton of grapes in a relatively short period of time. I don't like it because there is no quality control of the grapes, but wineries, like all of us, have to do what they've got to do.

With handpicking, the winery has actual people picking the grapes and making sure what is being picked is healthy. There's no downside to it, except that it costs the winery, and subsequently us consumers, more. But this is something I am personally fine paying for—not only does it lead to better wine, but it leads to more jobs.

Much like while the United States' Santa is sleighing, the Australia Santa is surfing;* the hemispheres have different harvesting seasons. For the northern hemisphere, harvest is between August and September, and for the southern hemisphere, it's February through April. Picking can occur during the day or at night; however, there are advantages to harvesting grapes at night, mainly because of the temperature. Not

---

* I'm kidding!

only is it cooler for workers who are putting in long hours of manual labor in the brutal summer months, but the lower temperature stabilizes grape sugars, making them firmer, easier to pick, and less likely to break. Because most grapes need to be cooled before fermentation, it saves the wineries time, money, and energy when the grapes come in at a cooler temperature from the vineyard.

No matter how you choose to harvest, the end result is you have a shit ton of grapes in bins. Grapes in bunches, grapes that are loose, grapes that still have all their stems, and whatever else from the vineyard has made it in there. The grapes are then sorted by varietal.

Varietal is a word people in wine use for "a single type of grape." Examples of varietals* include Cabernet Sauvignon, Pinot Grigio, Zinfandel, Sémillon, and virtually every single grape that can produce wine. Specific grapes work better in certain regions and climates than in others, although what varietals and how many different varietals a vineyard decides to work with is entirely up to them. Some wineries choose to just focus on one grape, while others have multiple varietals they work with. Grown in long rows, each varietal has its own section. You're not going to find four Grenache vines and then six Cabernet Franc vines all hanging out together.

But I digress, an easy thing to do when it comes to wine. The point is, you don't want the Merlot grapes crushed with the Riesling grapes, so they must be sorted.

---

* Some people say the plural *varietals* is not proper, and use *varieties*. I feel there can be varieties of anything and prefer to take poetic license with *varietals* to make it wine-grape specific. Just in case you, too, get in a fight with some asshole in Spain over semantics, now you are prepared.

But What about Blends?

A blend wine, made up of two or more different varietals, can be made one of two ways. Some winemakers blend the varietals in the steel tank before fermentation, a practice called co-fermentation. Other winemakers ferment each varietal separately and then blend small batches of the wine in different ratios until they achieve the desired flavor profile. They then use this ratio to create large batches of the blends.

After the grapes have been harvested and sorted, they are usually destemmed. I say "usually" because depending on the wine and the maturity of the stems, a winemaker may choose not to destem them. Stems are very high in **tannins**, the biomolecules that create the cotton-mouth feeling in red wines and can be good for certain wines that are meant to age. That said, grape skins and seeds already have high concentrations of tannins, so for most wines, the grapes are destemmed.

The grapes are then crushed, either by a machine aptly called a crusher, or manually by a good old-fashioned grape-stomping session, *I Love Lucy*–style. Imagine having clusters of grapes under your feet and stomping them vengefully, like you're vowing to make someone pay for wronging your family in a nineties thriller starring Denzel Washington. By the end, you'd be covered in juice, with your toes full of grape mash. That's how it's done manually. A crusher does that, too (with fewer quests of retribution), creating vats of straight-up grape sludge with its skins, pulp, and juice all mixed together. This chunky mishmash is called **the must**.

And this is where grapes go their separate ways, to become the wines they've always dreamed of being. Some red, some white, some perhaps even a dreamy rosé or an offbeat orange. It would be easy to assume that the varietal is what makes a wine look and taste the way it does, but in all actuality, the grape has very little to do with it. Much of a wine's flavor and color results from its treatment during different parts of the winemaking process, such as maceration.

Maceration is the soaking and softening of grape skins with their juice. If it wasn't for maceration, wine wouldn't have any color, because the juice itself is clear. For white wines, the grapes are pressed and the skins are out of there quicker than a one-night stand. But for red wines, the grapes are pressed and then basically spend the entire weekend—or even weeks—unabashedly cuddling with the skins. Awww, great for them! I love their love!

The Color Purple, Red, Green, & Yellow

Grape skins and their color are highly influential in the winemaking process. Red wines are made with grapes that are generally red, purple, or black, and white wines are usually made with grapes that are green, yellow, or even a little gray.

RED WINES

After being crushed, a red wine's must goes straight into steel fermentation tanks. Because red wine is fermented in its must, its juice takes on the red, purple, and black qualities of the grape skins that are chilling with it. Fermenting in its must also enhances the wine's aromas, flavors, and tannins, making those dry, bold reds you love so much with dinner.

In these fermentation tanks, yeast converts sugar into alcohol and carbon dioxide. Low-intervention winemakers rely solely on wild yeasts naturally existing on their grapes to do this on their own, but many winemakers add cultured yeasts to control the rate of fermentation and add flavor. Since all yeasts are natural, it's not that these cultured yeasts are artificial, but they aren't native to the environment. It's like buying instant yeast to make bread: Yeah, it's yeast, but still you bought it at a Kroger for a quick fix. Don't expect it to taste like the sourdough of the bread makers, who use yeast from their own starter.

I like to think of the yeast like Pac-Man munching up all the sugar and leaving a trail of alcohol and carbon dioxide behind him. While alcohol is obviously a good thing in wine, carbon dioxide is not. These bubbles push all skins to the top of the fermentation tank as the gases are being released, creating a cap on the juice. This is problematic because if those skins aren't mingling with the juice throughout the tank, you're missing out on all the must's benefits to the wine's color and flavors.

To get rid of that gas, winemakers employ punch-downs

and pump-overs, two more totally unembellished cellar terms. A **punch-down** is when a winemaker pushes the cap down from the top of the tank and stirs the tank by hand with a tool that looks like an oversize potato masher. A **pump-over** is when they hook a hose up to the bottom of the tank and pump the juice over the cap to mix it in. Which technique a winemaker uses, and how often, is totally up to them. Fermentation and its subsequent gas management can last days or weeks, depending on how long it takes for the yeast to eat all the sugar.

It's worth noting that rather than this traditional fermentation, some red wines go through the process of **carbonic maceration**. Instead of being crushed, full bunches of red grapes are put into fermentation tanks with carbon dioxide, causing individual grapes to begin fermentation from inside their grape skins, eventually getting crushed under their own weight. Made famous by the region of Beaujolais, this is how you get Gamay and other red varietals superfresh and poppy tasting.

No matter how fermentation goes down, the tanks are drained and the leftover must is pressed to squeeze out every last delicious drop. The juice is then placed in whatever container the winemaker wants to age it in, for however long the winemaker wants to age it. If they choose steel tanks or concrete eggs, they put it in there and let it get to aging, but if a winemaker decides to age the red wine in a barrel, there're a few more steps.

Barrel-aged wines, particularly oak-barrel-aged wines, go through **malolactic fermentation**. During this process, a wine hangs out in its barrel while all those tart cranberry or sour apple notes found in young red wines mellow into milder, creamier fruit notes. It's the difference between sour strawberry Starbursts and strawberries and cream Starbursts. Both are strawberry, both are delicious, but there's a difference in taste.

Barrel-aged wines also need to go through a process called **racking**. Because these barrels have been chilling in the cellars and lying on their sides while malolactic fermentation is going on, all the extra sediment settles at the bottom. Racking is when a winemaker lets the sediment sink to the bottom, and then syphons the free juice (sans sediment) into a new barrel to continue aging. Racking happens as often as the winemaker sees fit, usually every one to three months.

Some winemakers choose to filter their wine to remove more sediment before bottling, while others prefer just to go straight to the bottle. Unfiltered wines tend to be cloudy and have more sediment, although whether or not it affects the flavor of a wine is up for debate. Personally, I have found many unfiltered wines taste fresher and tarter, but it truly depends on the wine and the drinker. Either way, these wines are bottled, shipped out, bought, and poured straight into my mouth.

WHITE WINES

It doesn't take much outside of looking at a white wine to know it's different from a red wine, and you'd be right to assume that the process it undergoes in fermentation differs, too. While a red wine ferments with its must to get its hue and taste, a white wine quickly ditches its must to go its own way. The juice has little, if *any*, quality time with its skins before it is placed into tanks for racking, which is why white wines are light in color. After its sediment drops to the bottom during racking, the juice is then filtered out and put into another tank for fermentation.

Fermentation is still going to happen in its Pac-Man-like way, the yeasts eating sugar, converting it to alcohol and carbon dioxide. But because white wine is separated from its must before fermentation, winemakers leave their potato mashers and fire hoses at home. The rest of the process is just like how red wines are produced. Unbarreled white wines do their thing and age in tanks, concrete eggs, or amphorae (clay pots), and then they are bottled. Similarly, white wines that are barrel aged go through the same process as barrel-aged red wines: Juice is put in barrels, racked to remove extra sediment, aged, and finally bottled. It is then released, coming soon to a refrigerator near you.

ROSÉ

People tend to think that rosé is made from a specific kind of grape, but rosé is made just like red—using any red wine grapes and the maceration method (aka the with-skins way). The wine turns pink depending on how much time the juice is left with the skins, so your end result can be anything from heavy magenta to Himalayan sea-salt hues.

There are also two, lesser-used methods, and although they are much rarer, I can't have you going out in the world, drinking bomb-ass rosés, only to find yourself in a conversation with some jerky "rosé aficionado" who is like, "What do you *mean* you don't know what *saignée* is?" **Saignée** is a method where a producer is making a straight-up red wine, and then bleeds off some of the juice early in fermentation. With less juice in the tank, the wine has more contact with skins, creating deeper reds. The rosy-colored juice that was bled off is then fermented on its own to create rosé. This happens most commonly in Provence, France, with wines like Mourvèdre and Syrah. Rosé can also be made by **blending** a little red wine into white wine, but this is primarily a sparkling wine thing that you will find in places like Champagne. After that, it undergoes the same process as red wines and white wines: the whole barreling and racking versus not barreling and racking. Got it? Yeah, you do!

ORANGE WINES

Despite the name, orange wines are not made from oranges. They're white wines that are made like red wines—with the juice fermenting with the skins from anywhere between a couple days to many months. Often referred to as "skin-contact" wines, they can be anywhere from straw gold to vibrant orange in color. This length of time with the skins also gives orange wines characteristics similar to red wines, big in body and dry with more tannic structure, though they maintain the acidity of white wines. That being said, they taste nothing like red wines or white wines. Orange wines have a whole other realm of flavor that spans from bruised apples to sour beer.

SPARKLING WINE

It doesn't take a New Year's party to know that sparkling wine is special. From its iconic cork pop to its strings of tiny bubbling pearls, sparkling wine is glittering and giddy, which is why it's the wine of choice for celebratory occasions and spraying in hot tubs. Anyone who has had more than one glass of sparkling wine in their life can tell you that not all sparkling wines are made the same. Which is true, because there're actually four different ways.

Traditional Method (*Méthode Traditionnelle*)

Traditional Method is what put Champagne on the map, although this method is also used for other types of sparkling wine, like Cava and Franciacorta. In the Traditional Method, winemakers take the base wine that has already been fermented (sometimes it's a blend of multiple base wines, called a **cuvée**) and put it in bottles with more yeast and sugar to begin another round of fermentation, called **tirage**. These bottles are then sealed with crown caps (the cap you find on beer and the good old-fashioned Coca-Cola bottles) to trap the carbonation. They are then aged for a certain period of time before being **riddled**, a confusing word for placing the bottles tilting downward and regularly rotating them so all the dead yeast, or **lees**, settles in the neck of the bottle.

The bottles are then disgorged, which isn't as violent as it sounds (although still volatile when done manually).

Disgorgement is a form of filtration. Once all the lees settle in the neck of the bottles during riddling, they are then put in freezing brine so that the lees freeze and can be removed later by taking off the crown cap and letting the bubbles pop them out. The bottles are then **dosed**, or topped off with some wine and sugar, before being corked and made ready for rap videos or just regular brunch-time imbibing.

Tank Method

Also known as Charmat Method, this is widely used, especially for Prosecco, and is not nearly as complicated as Traditional Method. Basically, the winemaker is like, "Yo, let's take that base wine out of the tank and then put it in *another tank* for the second fermentation." Like tirage but without individual bottles, sugar and yeast are added to the second fermentation tank. Rather than being riddled and disgorged, the wines are filtered before being dosed and bottled.

Transfer Method

It's just like Traditional Method, except that after tirage, the bottles are filtered in another tank rather than being riddled and disgorged. This is primarily used for wines in giant, large-format bottles you're rarely, if ever, going to drink. I mean, have you ever drank out of a jeroboam? Because I sure haven't.

To Magnums, and Beyond!

Ever see a wine bottle bigger than your kid brother? That's a large-format bottle. Large-format bottles are custom-made for producers, so if you see one, you know that winemaker really loves and believes in that wine. Large-format bottles are known for aging because their ratio of air to wine is smaller than in 750ml bottles, meaning they oxidize slower and stay fresher longer.

> ➤ Magnum (1.5L) = 2 Bottles of Wine, 10 Glasses
> ➤ Double Magnum (3L) = 4 Bottles of Wine, 20 Glasses
> ➤ Jeroboam (4.5L) = 6 Bottles of Wine, 30 Glasses
> ➤ Imperial (6L) = 8 Bottles of Wine, 40 Glasses,
> ➤ Salmanazar (9L) = 12 Bottles of Wine, 60 Glasses
> ➤ Balthazar (12L) = 16 Bottles of Wine, 80 Glasses
> ➤ Nebuchadnezzar (15L) = 20 Bottles of Wine, 100 Glasses

Pétillant Naturel

Lovingly referred to as Pét-Nat, the cutest nickname ever, Pétillant Naturel used to be considered a rare and primitive way of making sparkling wine, but in recent years it's been making a comeback. Which, thank God, because the wines it produces are deliciously tart with soft bubbles. Pét-Nat is unique, because unlike other sparkling wines, which require two rounds of fermentation, Pét-Nat only uses one. Halfway through its first fermentation, the wine is bottled with a crown cap. There are no added sugars or yeast because as the juice finishes its fermentation in the bottle, there is nowhere for the carbon dioxide to escape to, and so the wine becomes bubbly.

THE ROLE OF A WINEMAKER

Each of these processes is extremely important to wine-making, but not as important as how a winemaker decides to use them. Each winemaker is like a scientist-artist who uses these tools and techniques to create a unique expression of their grapes. Since this is my book and I get to choose the analogies we'll use, let's say winemakers are like the Beatles. The Beatles didn't invent music. They didn't even invent the type of music they played. But it was how they played it, how they produced it, how they performed it that made it so special.

Let's take the song "Till There Was You" as an example. This track is originally from *The Music Man*, an aptly named musical that you probably have never seen if I haven't (and I did a *loooot* of musical theater growing up). I'm sure *The Music Man* is great, but I've watched some videos of the musical performance of "Till There Was You" and it's beautiful but totally not my kind of jam. I would not be caught dead attempting to sing it. But the Beatles' cover of "Till

There Was You" is a song I belt out every morning in my kitchen in my underwear, doing the dishes. It's Paul's sweetness, George's banging guitar solo, and Ringo maybe doing the best drumming of his life on those bongos that make it stick to my soul. The song is the same, but the interpretation is entirely unique.

It reminds me of Chardonnay. For a long time, all the Chardonnay I had ever tried tasted the same: thick and buttery, like the Pillsbury Doughboy's piss. I hated it with every taste bud in my mouth, avoided it like poison, and spoke very unkindly of it to anyone who would listen. But then I visited Scribe Winery in Sonoma in 2013. Although I was a huge fan of their reds, I was still scared of oak-bombed bottles of white. When it came time to taste their skin-fermented Chardonnay, I remember thinking—no, praying—"Just smile. Please, just smile." I'm terrible at hiding my feelings, and the last thing in the world I wanted to do was offend one of my favorite wineries. I took a sip.

And I didn't gag.

I didn't even frown.

Their skin-fermented Chardonnay was unlike anything I had ever tasted before. Where I had expected nauseating cream and fruit, there was punchy citrus and tropical nuances. There was a medium body but with a yearning dryness. In fact, there were bells. On a hill. That I had never heard ringing. And birds in the sky that I had never even fucking seen winging!

That day, I drank my words. I had condemned an entire varietal out of ignorance. It never crossed my mind that Chardonnay grapes didn't naturally taste like vanilla and butter, that someone made them taste that way. I'd been running my mouth about how terrible it was, when in all reality, Chardonnay was an innocent grape that got caught up in the wine game. It wasn't its fault a bunch of assholes in the nineties started prioritizing the flavor of oak over the actual wine, and the style has hung around in our supermarkets ever since.

This was one of the most important and formative experiences in my wine drinking. It humbled me, and took me from *ABC* across the belly (Anything But Chardonnay) to being open-minded and curious about all wine. And most important, it made me understand, respect, and admire the role of the winemaker.

Because wine isn't just grapes: It's what someone *does* with those grapes that makes it worth singing about.

Dude. We did it.

Phewf!

[*Wipes sweat from brow.*]

How wine is made is tough stuff, even when you're only scratching the surface of the subject. I didn't mention it at the top of the chapter because I didn't want you thinking it was boring shit you could skip. Not saying you're that kind of person, but *I am* that kind of person. I'm a lazy hedonist, and definitely would have just skimmed through it and gotten to the "fun stuff." But you can't do that with wine. To fully enjoy the "fun stuff," you have to understand the fundamental stuff first.

Luckily, we don't have to worry about it because you crushed this chapter like whole clusters of Carignan.

To-Drink List:

1. Go to the wine store.
2. Get two bottles of the same varietal but from two different producers, one oaked and one unoaked.
3. Don't be afraid to ask for help! That's what the people are there for, I promise.
4. Taste a glass of each wine side by side.
5. Taste the rainbow! Just kidding, taste how different the wines are. Oak has a very distinct flavor, making it easy to taste how much different winemaking techniques can affect the exact same grape.

CHAPTER THREE

What the Funk: Biodynamic, Organic, & Natural Wines

There's no doubt you've heard these buzzwords around wine shops, bars, and even at the grocery store. While these wines may seem to be a fad trying to chase after craft beer, organic produce, and shopping locally, it is actually a return to the ancestral winemaking practices that were used for centuries before the commercialization of wines. The good old days, when no one had to worry about rat's blood or fish bladder in their wines. Yes, you read that correctly, and I'm sorry in advance because this chapter is probably going to ruin your go-to $4 bottle. But it will also teach you what terms like *organic* and *natural* really mean, why commercial wines are totally gross, and why you can't care about where your kale comes from and not care about where your wine comes from.

I didn't mean to fall in love with natural wines. I didn't even know they were a thing. All I knew was that an importer named

Cory Cartwright and I followed each other on Twitter, and he was hosting a tasting at a wine shop I'd heard of, Domaine LA. And I was going.

It was early 2013, and my interest in wine outside of chugging cheap shit was still in its infancy. I'd never tasted anything like the wines Cory was pouring. The Duplessis Chablis tasted of limestone pool coping and honeysuckle, the Maison PUR Beaujolais Nouveau was a lightning bolt of cranberry concentrate, and Les Capriades Piège à Filles rosé sparkler was like pomegranate chiffon, each imported by the company Cory cofounded, Selection Massale. I didn't know wines could be so light bodied but have so much flavor, with acidity that tap-danced its way across my tongue. It felt like the scene in *Pleasantville* when the mom masturbates in the tub for the first time in her life and starts seeing color. You can't go back to a black-and-white, pleasureless existence with $6 wines that taste like Edible Arrangements and rotting beauty products after that.

I became obsessed with shopping at Domaine LA, looking for more of Selection Massale's imports, asking for anything like it and devouring it all at an ungodly pace that my Chase checking account could barely keep up with. It was like the heavens had opened and God (played by Jeff Goldblum) came to me with armfuls of French reds. "Marissa, I made these wines *just for you*," he purred as the Beach Boys' "Good Vibrations" rained down from the clouds. It was everything I loved, together, in a way I never even fathomed was possible. Sour and salty and gritty and poppy, they tasted like sour candy and potato chips! IN WINE!

That whole time, I had no idea I was drinking "natural wine."

I thought I was just finally spending more than $10 on a bottle.

While my love for natural wines started as selfishly as any of my other drinking did, it slowly but surely became so much more. Each bottle I researched to review became a rabbit hole, every question answered begging another. *What does* biodynamic *mean? Well, if the winery is making a point to farm without chemicals, does that mean other farms do farm with chemicals? Wait, THERE'S ALSO CHEMICALS IN THE WINE?!*

Yes, farms use chemicals, and yes, there are chemicals in your wine. *A lot* of them. And this is why I drink natural wines today. Because I believe that being as kind to the environment as possible is extremely important, especially as the problem of climate change continues to grow and environmental progress is being prevented by people with monetary stakes in the status quo. Because I believe wines should always speak to the grapes and the land, not be rotten, orchard trash juice pumped full of chemicals to taste "like wine." Because natural wines are better for the Earth, and they are better for the consumer.

And because they taste like tart plum bubblegum drizzled with strawberry balsamic and dusted with chalk. I'm not going to pretend that isn't still important to me. It is, but not nearly as important as it is to support small wine producers with good practices in and out of the cellar.

That said, you will never catch me throwing a fit in a

restaurant, belaboring dinner party hosts over their selections, or pulling a soapbox out of my purse when everyone's at the bar just trying to have a good time. Nor will you find me turning down a beautiful, well-crafted, and cared-for bottle of wine because it's not technically to a T "natural." My attitude is the same with the natural wine movement as it is with everything in wine: I am not interested in judging or shaming or lecturing anyone; I'm interested in drinking good wine, having a good time, and giving you the information you need to make good decisions.

BUT WHAT DOES IT ALL MEAN?! CLARIFYING THE TERMS

You've for sure stumbled upon bottles being marketed with organic grapes, saw a new banner for "Natural Wines" hanging in your Whole Foods, or grabbed a bottle with a sticker promoting sustainability. These phrases may sound like you've pulled a page out of the thesaurus, but they are about as interchangeable as *your* and *you're*. Not knowing how to distinguish between organic and biodynamic probably won't leave you looking foolish on the Internet, but it will leave you confused at the wine shop. Here are the definitions to know when buying noncommercial wines.

Organic wines are much like organic foods in that they are government regulated and certified that no artificial chemicals, fertilizers, pesticides, fungicides, or herbicides have been used while growing the grapes. In the United States, a certified organic wine means it has been made from organically grown grapes and has no added sulfites. In Europe, a certified organic wine has been made from organically grown grapes but may have added sulfites. It's not uncommon to come across a wine that is "made with organic grapes" but is without certification.

Biodynamic wines are not government regulated but do follow a very strict agricultural and spiritual ritual based on the ideology of Austrian philosopher Rudolf Steiner. While it incorporates all the anti-chemical vibes of organic farming, biodynamic farming is also about treating the vineyard as an entire ecosystem that must be kept in balance. This balance is kept through an intricate mix of special field and compost preparations, which often sound like pagan rituals straight out of an advanced edition of *The Teen Spell Book*. As in, you need to take steps like spraying valerian flower juice all over your compost, and burying horns stuffed with manure and digging them up at certain points in the lunar cycles.

Natural wines are also unregulated, and the term is ambiguous. Generally, it means that the grapes are grown without chemicals or pesticides, are dry-farmed and handpicked, and use only native yeast. They have no additives and no fining agents, and use little to no filtering or sulfites. Nothing is added, and nothing is taken away.

Sustainable wines are usually organically farmed. The term mostly refers to steps the winery itself has taken to be environmentally and socially responsible, including energy and water conservation.

"Low-Intervention" Wines

There are many wineries that make wine with as little outside influence as possible but don't fit into any of the aforementioned categories. They may be entirely organic but don't have the money to be certified. Maybe they only add minimal sulfites to the wines they feel benefit from it, but then it excludes them from organic certification. Perhaps they play a little loose with biodynamic farming and can't be classified "biodynamic" but are basically biodynamic. *The term* low-intervention *is a catchall for these wines*, and means that the winemaker is doing the absolute minimum to their wines, even if they can't come out and say they are this or that. You're putting your trust in the winemaker, that even if they add sulfites or don't plant based on the moon, you trust that they are making choices to make the best product while still being as natural as possible.

Generally, the profile of organic, natural, and biodynamic wines is light to medium bodied (although you can find big-bodied, high-ABV natural wines, too!) with high acidity. Because there are no additives, the character of these wines is heavily terroir driven. Their texture varies from gritty to smooth, depending on filtering, as does their cloudiness. Most often, these wines are meant to be drank very young, and should not be aged without talking to your merchant.

HOW DRINKING COMMERCIAL WINE IS A LOT LIKE "DATING" IN YOUR EARLY TWENTIES

I didn't really "date" in my early twenties. In fact, I'm pretty sure the word *dating* was made up only to spare me the embarrassment of having to say things to my mom like "Yeah, I've been sleeping with this surfer for a couple weeks, and I like him a lot, although we never really talk. He only wants to smoke weed and watch *Hustle & Flow.*"

We've all had those "relationships" in our lives, whether it is aforementioned surfers who can't see past the end of their joints, the brunch-obsessed with a flair for the dramatic, or that asshole from the bar you still get a late-night "Hey" from once every three months. For me, it was mostly musicians who were physically incapable of texting before midnight. Sure, we never saw each other in daylight, except getting breakfast burritos at the truck outside their house the next morning as I walked heels in hand to my car, but whatever. We were sleeping together for like four months! Plus, I went to all their shows! Plus, they invited me to the afterparties! Sometimes. In my mind, it was always a match made in Los Angeles indie-rock-scene heaven. It was easy to ignore that they were unemployed, only wanted blowjobs, and always smelled like cigarettes, because they told that one great joke, wore that one great shirt, and loved that one Wes Anderson movie. Because I was twenty-two, I didn't know I deserved better than some one-note dickhead.

Commercial wine is the same one-note dickhead.

If you doubt me, let me tell you about a wine I used to "drink." He's really popular, and I'm sure you've heard of him. Not to get weird, but we've both probably had him in our mouth. I don't want to name him by name, because that is rude and unprofessional, so let's call him Chuck.

When I was in my early twenties, I was super into Chuck, but I wasn't really ever *drinking* Chuck. I was chugging him. I wasn't spending quality time with him. I wasn't taking the time to really look at him, really smell him, really taste him. And when I *did* take the time to really look at him, really smell him, really taste him, I didn't really like him. Kind of like the guys I was "dating." The musicians looked like musicians, they smelled like musicians, and they played "music." Did I particularly enjoy their company? No, but sleeping with a guitarist seemed like more fun than *not* sleeping with a guitarist. Chuck looks like wine, smells like wine, and tastes like "wine." Did I particularly enjoy drinking it? No, but chugging wine was more fun than not chugging wine.

But at some point, you begin to notice things that make you question your judgment. This person you're "dating," yeah, they have seemingly never washed their sheets. Ever. Or better yet, they never had sheets to begin with, just a Christmas-patterned fleece blanket on top of a bare mattress you were too drunk to realize was supersketchy. The more time you spend with this person you're "dating," the more you find out how gross they are. It's the same thing with mass-produced, commercial wine, my friends. Under that familiar label is a load of chemicals and additives covering up a bunch of bullshit, and a lot of crushed-up birds. Yes. You read that correctly. CRUSHED-UP BIRDS. And insects, rats, squirrels, and a ton of other animals that naturally live in the areas where vineyards are mass-harvested. If you think for a second that big wine producers are any different from the big corporations that your hippie best friend from college keeps posting about on Facebook, you are sorely mistaken. Commercial wine producers take a mechanical grape-harvesting machine with rubber rods that beat the vines, dropping whatever shakes loose onto a conveyor belt and into a holding bin. Yes, the batches are eventually filtered, but not before a tractor throws a fox into the lot! Okay, fine. Maybe there aren't that many dead foxes in your wine. But this method harvests eighty to two hundred tons of grapes a day, and a lot of MOG (materials other than grapes, like crushed birds), so chances are, you've probably consumed at least a little dead fox.

For the sake of argument, let's say that these harvesting machines aren't picking up random forest creatures. Well, they're still collecting plenty of grapes that there is no quality control over. Unripe, unhealthy, or rotted grapes are still being picked and pressed into the wine. These large loads of collected grapes also put delicate grape skins at risk to be broken and become oxidized, which turns wine brown and makes it taste like vinegar. If you think that it's all going to be okay because they put them in fancy oak barrels, you are again wrong. They take the wine to a District 9–esque compound and put it in huge steel tanks, like a Budweiser factory off the 210 freeway.

If you're totally chill with blood and rotting fruit, how do you feel about arsenic? As in the poison that can straight-up kill people? A lawsuit filed by wine consumers in March 2015 brought to light a study by BeverageGrades that showed that twenty-eight California wineries were using up to 500 percent more arsenic than is considered safe by the Environmental Protection Agency (EPA). Although there are plenty of goods that have natural arsenics, these were not natural arsenics. They were classified as "inorganic arsenics," meaning someone put them there.

And this isn't news. Every fifteen years or so, this information hits the media. Everyone freaks out, then forgets, then goes back to their wine-drinking habits, then fifteen years later they are completely shocked again. The chemical additives in wine (and not just California wine, but international wines as well) have been reported since the 1960s. Way back in 1968, it was discovered that some Italian wines weren't quite wine—they were concoctions of bottom-of-the-barrel wine leftovers, beet sugar, potassium ferrocyanide, well water, ox blood, and ethyl chlorocarbonate. Basically, they were the Natty Lights of wine.

Today, there can be dozens of chemicals in wine. There are no regulations in law to make companies tell you this, but as your friend, I think you should know. If the FDA made commercial wineries list everything that is in their wine, it would read like the back of a Gatorade bottle. The most common additives in wine are sulfur dioxide (sulfites), ascorbic acid (vitamin C), clay, acid, sugar, cultured yeasts, gelatin, charcoal, egg product, casein, and isinglass, a collagen taken from dried fish bladders. And that's only naming a few of these foreign ingredients.

Our bodies aren't built to handle all these chemicals and additives. Those gnarly "wine" hangovers have nothing to do with wine, and everything to do with the fact that people are chugging back two-liter sodas' worth of chemicals in a single evening. No shit your friend would call out of work if she got crazy and took a few party-size Sprites to the dome, no matter how many glasses of water you made her drink in between liters. Our bodies also can't process these chemicals and additives like they do natural ingredients. While carbs and sugar obviously aren't the best for staying fit, if you're active, your body will use them for energy. But your body can't do anything with these chemicals and additives, so it stores them.

It's no wonder, with all that bullshit thrown in and corners cut, that commercial wines taste as fresh and delicious as a thin, soggy, fast-food dollar burger that has condensed into an unintelligible mass of mystery meat and sugar. Have you noticed that those wines have one solid flavor that hits the front of your tongue and that's it? That's because it's not good. It doesn't have a flavor profile, it just has *a flavor*: "Wine." Because it's chemically constructed to taste like "wine." Great wines, just like great partners, should stimulate you all over. They should stimulate your brain and your creativity and all sorts of things, but most important, they should stimulate your mouth. From the tip of your tongue to the back of your palate, you should feel them. Did that come off sexual? Good. It should. You wouldn't keep dating someone who just has one mediocre move in bed, and you shouldn't keep drinking wine that just tastes like "wine."

I'm not here to shame you for drinking commercial wine. No one rolls out into the world and starts dating their soul mate and drinking the finest Bordeaux. We all start "dating" and "drinking" somewhere, and more often than not, it's in a bedroom the size of a shoe box, with three bottles of Shaw and zero wineglasses. And that's okay! But I hope you can see how these wines are bad for you in a much different way than D.A.R.E. led us to believe.

IF YOU CARE ABOUT YOUR MICROGREENS, YOU SHOULD CARE ABOUT YOUR WINE

At the bottom of my street in Silverlake, there is a farmers' market every Saturday. Waking up on the weekend and walking down the hill to grocery shop is one of my favorite things in the world to do. My husband and I have this whole ritual. We get our forty-ounce canteen filled with iced coffee from the couple with the coffee shop across the neighborhood, me always hoping they brought the baby. We then go to our produce guy. There's a couple produce guys, but the one we go to has our favorite selection of greens and the most fragrant bushels of rosemary, and never makes me feel stupid when I ask which one is the parsley and which one is the cilantro.* Our fingers are always crossed that the mushroom guy is there, but he hasn't been lately, although we do enjoy conversations with the fish guy about sustainable, eco-friendly choices. I usually end up running off to the flower booth on the other end of the market, and grab armfuls of color for the

---

* I should know the difference by now, and I do! Just not when it's 9:00 A.M. and I'm totally stoned, which is the only way I go to the market.

price of six tulips at the grocery store, to take home and turn into a bouquet while listening to Django Reinhardt. And we always, always get tamales to take home for lunch. The family-run stand is helmed by a young teenage daughter, and clusters of junior-high boys loiter around, playfully teasing her in between customers.

And I just love it. I love the fresh produce, and I love this little community: the farmer who handles his squash blossoms as gently as the couple making coffee rock their baby; the fisherman that fucking hates how everyone loves salmon so much; the young girl who manages her family's tamale stand when she probably would rather be sleeping in. It is important to me to support them and their small businesses, to contribute to my local economy and support environmentally conscious and chemical-free agriculture. That is why I shop at my farmers' market. And I think that is why most people shop at their farmers' markets, too. Because they care about what they put in their bodies, how the land is treated, and supporting local and small businesses.

This is why it is mind-boggling to me how often I will be at the farmers' market and hear people fawning over their microgreens, or leeks, or whatever vegetable they saw in last month's *Bon Appétit*, and lamenting over the use of pesticides, GMOs, and water waste in industrialized agriculture, and then walk into the liquor store on the corner and come out with a bottle of the cheapest domestic sparkling wine that is in every grocery store in America as we speak.

Most people don't think about wine like they think about food, but it's important that we all start doing so. Just like precious baby gem lettuces and radicchio, wine is an agricultural product, and mass-produced, commercial wines are often made with grapes grown in the same ways we shun in the produce aisle.

Drinking natural wines votes for better agricultural practices with your dollars, just like buying that fennel from the farmers' market does. It supports wine producers who don't use pesticides, fungicides, or synthetic fertilizers that can contaminate water sources but farm soil organically, which absorbs more carbon dioxide. While organic farming alone isn't going to stop climate change, it's a step in the right direction and promotes healthy, natural ecosystems where native plants and animals can thrive. Natural wines are also dry-farmed, meaning they rely on natural rainfall rather than irrigation, and waste zero water.

Natural wines not only benefit the environment but also small businesses. Natural winemakers and producers are not the rich white guy who retired, bought a fleece vest one day, and decided his new hobby was making the same bullshit Napa Cabernet he's been drinking since the first Bush administration. These winemakers are small business owners. They are families who have put everything they have into making wine, and often still have day jobs, just like most people pursuing their dreams. The people making mass-produced wines are sitting pretty in a gaudy "château" somewhere, and purchasing their wine is like throwing a penny into their endless fountain of wealth. But for natural winemakers and producers, each bottle they sell can be the difference between whether or not they're able to keep the lights on.

I know how privileged I am to live in California and to have access to fresh produce and natural wines. But if we take organic food or even craft beer as an example, over the last ten years, those items have gone from rare to *everywhere.* It's because people wanted it, and they bought it. Natural wines are becoming more and more available, so next time you go shopping, give your wine selection as much thought as your microgreens.

Natural wine is just like any other wine. There are people who are definitely exploiting the trend, but there are also people who are passionate about making these wines even without making much money doing it. There are beautiful, well-made natural wines, and there are absolute shit natural wines (although a little more literal here because many natural wines have an aroma of "barnyard" about them). You have to just try them for yourself, which I think is very worth it when considering how much better for you, the land, and small producers they are.

To-Drink List:

1. Try at least one natural wine.
2. Write down your tasting notes and compare them with your go-to under-$10 bottle.
3. Tomorrow, take note of how surprisingly un-hungover you are and rejoice.

CHAPTER FOUR

Tasting Wine

Ah, yes, the moment you've been waiting for: drinking! Ahem, I mean, tasting. They definitely go hand in hand, but the difference between the two is the difference between playing catch and pitching. The movement may be similar, but one is a specific skill that requires a lot more practice. Same thing with tasting wine. You have to practice being present with your wines, practice focusing on specific sensations and flavors, and practice verbalizing those things. The good news is tasting wine is a hell of a lot easier than pitching (take it from someone who regularly cried on the mound and is still haunted by Tom Hanks yelling, "There's no crying in baseball!"). It's nothing you can't do as long as you actually start doing it and doing it often. Plus, you've got me to coach you play-by-play, always ready to give you a metaphorical congratulatory/consensual slap on the ass. Clear eyes, full glasses, can't lose!

Wine tasting often conjures thoughts of quiet tasting rooms with a handful of well-to-do white people who are slurping and murmuring things in slightly British-sounding accents like "I'm getting willow bark, John." John shakes his head and spits into a bucket with great velocity, saying, "No, no, *no*, Felicia. You're doing it wrong; you must swirl *counterclockwise.* And it's most definitely the bark of a s*ilver birch.*" And there I am in the corner, drinking my wine, trying to figure out their accents and why John is being such an asshole about Felicia's willow bark because who died and made John the king of deciphering different trees in wine, and above all, asking myself, "Where the hell are they getting bark? *Am I* supposed to be tasting bark? IS THERE BARK IN THIS WINE?!"

It's this type of pressure that causes many people to disregard the traditional tasting experience altogether. As much as I would like to tell you I discovered that the long-established wine-tasting technique of sniffing and swirling is a meaningless dog-and-pony show for the Johns of the world, I can't because it's not. As it turns out, these methods are extremely useful, but probably not for the reason you're thinking. Sniffing, swirling, and sipping don't develop extraordinary taste buds—you, me, and those dudes in sommelier documentaries all operate with the same stock senses we were born with. Instead, the process helps to develop a particular sensitivity toward wine tasting. Rather than directly affecting your senses, wine tasting is for your *brain*, because most of wine tasting is just *remembering* other wines you've tasted.

This sounds simple enough. *"I always remember the wines I like!"* you're thinking. But is it that simple? Sure, you liked the wine you had at dinner the other night, but do you remember specifically *why* you liked it? Was it your favorite shade of red? Did it smell like a high school crush? Did it taste like a favorite dessert? What was it even called? Most times, we can't say. And that's a bummer, because describing a wine as "the one I liked" doesn't help much when it comes to buying or ordering more of it. This is where tasting comes in handy. It's a conscious way of imbibing, taking mental notes so that you can remember what you like and, more important, drink more of what you like.

You don't need to wax poetic about every Pinot you get your hands on. No one wants to be *that guy*, the one that turns dinner parties into graveyard snoozefests with their talk of the "wine tips" they picked up while barbacking in Portland for three months. But it's important to remember that tasting wine isn't a superpower. **It's just paying attention**. With all the stress of our day-to-day lives, it's so rare that we are present in a moment and are paying attention to what is happening right in front of us rather than to what has happened or what is going to happen or who is posting what on where. The wine-tasting process forces us to be present and pay attention by isolating and addressing individual senses. Not only does it make you think about different aspects of a wine, but if you do it systematically, it is that much easier to remember. So put down your phone and grab a glass, because your wine isn't going to taste itself.

APPEARANCE

Unlike real life, where we have to suppress our natural desire to judge people by the shitty band T-shirts they wear, when it comes to wine, you are allowed and encouraged to make assumptions about a wine based on its looks. It is very freeing, because even if you're totally wrong, you still get to drink wine and no one's feelings get hurt. Giving a glass of wine a good up-and-down can be a great first step to figuring out what style of wine you're drinking.

As you learned when we were discussing winemaking, the color of a wine is dictated by how long the pressed grape juice has contact with its skins during maceration. The depth of the color is dependent on how thick the skins are. So a thin-skinned grape, like the ones that produce Pinot Noir, is going to create a lighter-hued wine, whereas the grapes for Cabernet Sauvignon have a thicker skin and create a much richer color.

In an ideal setting, to examine a wine's color, you should look down at it at a forty-five-degree angle against a white background. The true color of the wine is at the center of the glass, and tends to fade or change as it expands outward. But how often are you in some Instagram palace of white marble and walls? If there's no white around, don't trip. Still check for the color at a forty-five-degree angle, if possible, but if it's too dark, don't be afraid to raise the glass to the light and look through it at eye level.

When it comes to white wines, the lighter the color, the crisper and more refreshing the wine. If it's darker and more golden yellow, you can expect a fuller flavor profile that has probably been oak aged. If it looks brownish, it's oxidized—but that doesn't mean it's bad. Many natural wines are oxidized on purpose. If you're concerned about whether or not your wine is meant to be oxidized, talk to whoever sold it to you. Wines that are skillfully and purposefully oxidized can be delicious, but wines that are oxidized due to a flaw are gross, and you need your money back.

With red wines, the lighter the color, the brighter and tarter the wine. The darker the red, the bigger and bolder the wine. Much as with white wines, the darker the wine, the more likely they have been aging in oak.

But there are other factors that can tell you about a wine beyond just the color. You also want to look at the clarity of the wine. A cloudy wine is either a natural wine or wine gone bad. If you shop at a spot that is super into biodynamics and you get a cloudy wine, don't worry about it. If you buy a wine at a bodega and it is cloudy, you *probably* should pour it down the sink. Same with sediment. Sediment is totally normal in natural wines, but not so normal if you're drinking Sauvignon Blanc that you bought from the grocery store by your mom's house.

SWIRLING & SMELLING

Now that you've stared down your wine, it's time to give it the ol' swirl and sniff. The swirl and sniff should be like a slow dance: rhythmic, smooth, and unforced. Take that glass by the stem and give it a twirl. After a few turns, bring it in close and breathe in deeply, like your face is buried in the nape of the neck of your crush, who finally got drunk enough to give you the time of day. A good wine will leave you feeling just like that moment—like your heart is melting and your loins are exploding all at once. And some wines will leave you wondering how the hell you got stuck dancing with it, wishing it had worn deodorant, and praying you can escape without it making contact with your mouth.*

Swirling

Swirling is a lot like dancing in the sense that everyone has their own style, but you need a sense of rhythm and a bit of technique to not look like a total jackass, or worse, spill your wine, when you're doing it. You want to channel your inner Fred Astaire and subdue your Elaine Benes. It helps to have a couple steps mastered before you hit the floor (or bar), so here are the basic moves to get your swirl on.

The Table Swirl

1. Set your glass on a flat surface, such as a table, counter, or that one clean patch of your desk.

---

* That is the wine you end up marrying in the romantic-comedy adaptation of this book, by the way.

2. With your palm facing the table, hold the base of the stem between your index and middle fingers.
3. Apply pressure to the base and make small, smooth circular motions with your wrist.

The Wrist Swirl

1. Hold your glass by the stem, toward the base.
2. Gently swirl your glass like it's Hula-Hooping.
3. This doesn't have a third step, but it is actually harder than the table swirl, so don't get cocky or else you'll end up just rocking your wine back and forth and making everyone seasick.

It doesn't matter how you swirl, but trust me, you have to swirl. This isn't one of those DIY project steps you can skip, like, "Eh, I don't need the sequins." You always need to swirl (and really, you always need the sequins, let's be honest). First, swirling releases the wine's aromatic compounds. Wine has dozens of these compounds, formed via everything from acids and alcohols reacting, to bacteria, fermentation, and aging. Second, swirling your wine brings oxygen into the glass, softening tannins and acidity so it's more delicious to drink (and who doesn't want their wine to be more delicious?!). Once you start swirling, and you smell and taste how it affects your wine for the better, you'll never skip swirling again.

Nice Legs

Legs. Tears. Weird streaks on the side of your glass after you swirl it around. Whatever you call them, they aren't anything to be concerned with. The streaks have nothing to do with the quality of a wine, but instead are an indication of its alcohol content. The more alcohol in a wine, the more streaks, simple as that.

Smelling

So you and this wine have been dancing for a sec now, and it's time to nuzzle your face into it and breathe in its sweet, sweet perfume.

In my personal and professional opinion, smelling is the most important part of this process. Of course, tasting is the most fun, but your tongue can only actually taste five different sensations—sweet, sour, salt, bitter, and that mysterious umami. Flavor is the result of the smell of something combined with its taste. When you don't smell your wine before drinking it, it's like you've skipped the dance, have decided to forgo any sort of foreplay, and are going straight for boning a stranger in the bathroom. Yeah, you're getting smashed, but you haven't given yourself much to savor.

Smelling your wine is as simple as it sounds. You just smell it. No fancy technique or dance moves required. Everyone can do it.

People get tripped up when they believe that they have to smell their wine and immediately call out detailed descriptors. If you smell aged Italian leather in your wine, by all means, say so! But identifying aromas in wine is often difficult, and it can feel impossible to pick a single scent out of all the scents in all the world in your one glass of wine. Resist feeling overwhelmed when you're taking in a wine's bouquet, the swanky word for how it smells, by breaking the aromas down by category.

Wines' primary aromas fall into the following categories: fruit, earth, floral, green, and spice. Of course, there are variations and minutiae within each of these categories, but it makes it so much easier to pick out specific scents if you start by identifying these bigger notes and then narrowing it down from there. This way you're not saying, "Oh, shit, what does this smell like!? There are a million smells!" but rather, "I know it's going to smell like one or more of these things. I know what fruits smell like. I've got this." These primary aromas come straight from the grapes used in the wine, as well as the environment in which the grapes are grown.

In red wine, the fruit notes are red fruit and black fruit. Simple as that: cherry, cranberry, strawberry, raspberry, blackberry, blueberry, plum, and boysenberry. Honestly, if you've ever bought yourself PB&J supplies and have gone down the J aisle, you're going to kill it.

White wines feature fruit notes of citrus, tropical, and tree fruits. We're all pretty familiar with citrus—lemon, lime, grapefruit. Tropical fruits include pineapple, guava, passion fruit—really, anything that reminds you of being on an island getaway. *Tree fruit* is not that common a term outside the wine world, but it encompasses the other hanging fruits that can be found in white wines, like apples, peaches, pears, and nectarines.

Note: Ironically, you will never actually smell grapes in your wine.

Earthiness in wine evokes a scent of soil, dust, clay, gravel, and minerals, like slate or limestone. This comes from the environment in which the grapes were grown, or the terroir. This French word that I rarely say correctly, embodies all the environmental qualities from the vineyard, such as its soil, slopes, climate, plants, and mineral content. (PS: It's pronounced *tare-wah*.)

Floral notes can vary from a subtle spring breeze to straight-up perfume. Common floral notes include rose, lavender, violet, and gardenia.

Green notes include herbs like tarragon, thyme, and mint, and things like fresh-cut grass. It also includes vegetables like green bell pepper, jalapeño, and the very-ungreen-and-not-even-a-vegetable tomato.

Spice notes are most commonly black pepper or white pepper (not a joke about salt; white pepper is a real thing), but you'll also run across clove, cinnamon, nutmeg, and anise.

Wine also has secondary and tertiary aromas that come from fermentation and aging. Secondary aromas from fermentation are caused by microbes like yeast, which are often what give wines a "bready" or "creamy" smell. Tertiary aromas that come from aging are often aromas of tobacco or coffee. Wine aged in oak gives off aromas like vanilla or smoke.

Faults in wine also create certain smells. When a wine is defective, often from shitty storage or poor winemaking, it is considered to have a "fault." Without writing a chemistry book explaining why, let's just say it's best to be wary of anything that smells like wet dog or cardboard, musty attic, sulfur, burnt rubber, mold, or straight-up vinegar.

If you're saying to yourself, "Dude, how am I going to smell all this in wine?" I promise you, you can and you will. Now that you know what you're looking for, all you have to do is practice. And considering "practice" means "pouring yourself a glass of wine," I don't think you're going to have a problem fitting it into your schedule.

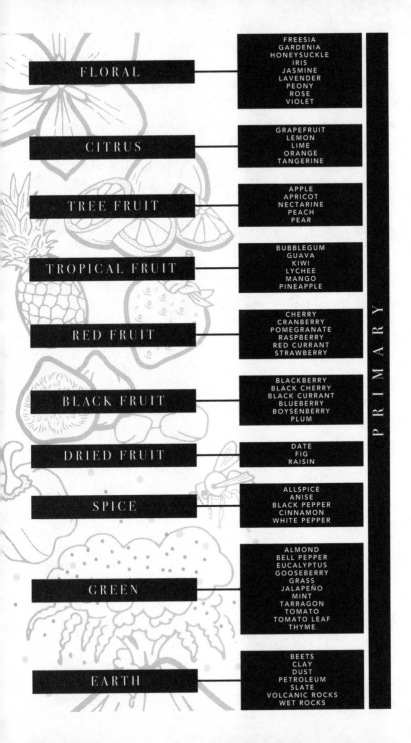

FLORAL
FREESIA
GARDENIA
HONEYSUCKLE
IRIS
JASMINE
LAVENDER
PEONY
ROSE
VIOLET

CITRUS
GRAPEFRUIT
LEMON
LIME
ORANGE
TANGERINE

TREE FRUIT
APPLE
APRICOT
NECTARINE
PEACH
PEAR

TROPICAL FRUIT
BUBBLEGUM
GUAVA
KIWI
LYCHEE
MANGO
PINEAPPLE

RED FRUIT
CHERRY
CRANBERRY
POMEGRANATE
RASPBERRY
RED CURRANT
STRAWBERRY

BLACK FRUIT
BLACKBERRY
BLACK CHERRY
BLACK CURRANT
BLUEBERRY
BOYSENBERRY
PLUM

DRIED FRUIT
DATE
FIG
RAISIN

SPICE
ALLSPICE
ANISE
BLACK PEPPER
CINNAMON
WHITE PEPPER

GREEN
ALMOND
BELL PEPPER
EUCALYPTUS
GOOSEBERRY
GRASS
JALAPEÑO
MINT
TARRAGON
TOMATO
TOMATO LEAF
THYME

EARTH
BEETS
CLAY
DUST
PETROLEUM
SLATE
VOLCANIC ROCKS
WET ROCKS

PRIMARY

SECONDARY

MICROBIAL
- BEER
- BUTTER
- CREAM
- MUSHROOM
- SOURDOUGH
- TRUFFLE

TERTIARY

OAK AGING
- CIGAR BOX
- COCONUT
- SMOKE
- VANILLA

GENERAL AGING
- COCOA
- COFFEE
- DRIED FRUIT
- LEATHER
- NUTS
- TOBACCO

FAULTS

TCA (CORKED)
- CARDBOARD
- OLD NEWSPAPERS
- WET DOG

SULFIDES
- BOILED EGGS
- BURNT MATCHES
- BURNT RUBBER
- CAT PEE

BRETTANOMYCES
- BARNYARD
- HAMSTER CAGE
- MANURE

COOKED
- OLD SHERRY
- STEWED FRUIT

VOLATILE ACIDITY
- BALSAMIC VINEGAR
- NAIL POLISH REMOVER

TASTING

FINALLY. THE MOMENT YOU'VE ALL BEEN WAIT-
ING FOR! PUTTING WINE IN YOUR MOUTH! But don't
get too excited. Yes, soon I will set you heathens free to pour
as much juice down your hatches as you damn well please.
But the tasting portion of wine tasting isn't just to drink
wine—it's how to evaluate the different sensations, textures,
and flavors you experience while drinking wine.

As I mentioned earlier, **your tongue can only taste
sweet, sour, salt, bitter, and umami**. If this brings back
memories of elementary school science diagrams of tongues
with designated areas for each taste, you can go ahead and
forget it. The tongue diagram was first introduced in 1901 by
a German scientist, Dieter P. Hanig. Although he was correct
that the tongue does detect these different flavors, and with
more sensitivity and taste buds around its edges, he was
wrong in his artistic interpretation of his findings. There isn't
one spot for sweet or sour or the others; you can feel these sensations all over your tongue.

That's why when describing wine, you hear people talk
about their **front, mid, and back palate**. Imagine your
tongue divided into thirds, horizontally. A good wine will
have different sensations across your entire tongue. By divid-
ing the tongue into these palates, it makes it easier to identify
the various sensations and textures, and you get to say things
like "This is soft and light on the front" or "Jesus Christ, this
has a whiskey back!"

When tasting wine, you want to take a nice-size sip,

but not a gulp. It's a sip, and not one of those "sips" your dude takes and then half of the soda is gone. You want enough to taste it, but not so much that you can't move it around in your mouth. Personally, I'm from the tasting school of Three Sips. I feel like that's enough sips to give a wine a chance and to evaluate the qualities and characteristics of the wine's taste.

Take a sip, think on it. Just get the general vibe of the wine. No pressure.

Take another sip, and maybe incorporate that weird slurping thing called **trilling**. Trilling is where you bring air into your mouth while the wine is still in there. This aerates the wine in your mouth, releasing more of the aromas, which helps define flavors. You totally don't have to do this, though, and I wouldn't recommend doing it at dinner or anything unless you want to look like an asshole. I only do it if I'm at a serious tasting or if I really care about the wine. But I feel that one day you're going to be tasting serious wine you care about, too, so it's good to know about this technique.

Take a third sip and chew it. Yep, I said chew your wine. Trust me—it's such an easy way to enhance your wine tasting. By chewing, it pushes the wine throughout the entirety of your mouth, hitting more taste buds and subsequently heightening many of the wine's taste qualities. Be warned: This can get intense. Something you thought was maybe a little bitter can quickly become a sweater made of spikes in your mouth. But the good news is it leaves you without a doubt as to the flavor and sensation, and perhaps introduces you to some element of the wine you may have overlooked completely.

These sips aren't for casually mulling over your opinion of the wine—you've got a whole bottle to do that. These sips are focused, as are you, to identify specific characteristics of the wine, such as sweetness, acidity, tannin, body, and texture.

Sweetness

If a wine is sweet, it's generally a white wine or a red dessert wine, and it will hit you like someone just sprayed Victoria's Secret Love Spell. Whether it's faint and far away or thicker than a perfume cloud after PE, it is unavoidable and undeniable. You *know* that shit. Same with a wine's sweetness. Sweetness in wine is caused by natural residual sugars from the grapes after fermentation (or adding sugar, a frowned-upon practice called chaptalization), and it will be one of the first things you notice about a wine. Quick myth busting: Sweet is not the same as fruity. Many people will say a ripe, fruit-forward red is "sweet," but it's just fruity. The best way to figure out if a wine is actually sweet or the fruit is throwing you off is to plug your nose and taste it. Fruity qualities come from the wine's aroma, whereas sweetness is a sensation on your tongue. If it still tastes sweet with your nose plugged, then you know it's actually sweet.

Acidity

Acidity in a wine is how sour it tastes, and it's this sensation that can leave your mouth watering. Think of the acidity scale like a candy aisle, with everything ranging from Warheads to Swedish Fish. **A high-acidity wine** is going to be tart and more like Sour Punch Straws, whereas **a low-acidity wine** is going to be creamier, like those smoothie-inspired Skittles.

Body

There's no doubt you've heard people talking about a wine being this-bodied or that-bodied. What they're talking about is the feeling of a wine's "weight" in your mouth. **A light-bodied wine** is going to feel thin, clean, or delicate, and go down like water. **A full-bodied wine** is going to feel heavy, dense, or powerful—kind of like trying to swallow a thick perfume. **A medium-bodied wine** is somewhere between the two ends of the spectrum, with light- to medium-bodied and medium- to full-bodied wines. Unlike wrestling, there are no specific regulations that define a wine's weight class. You just have to let it step onto the scale of your tongue and measure for yourself.

Texture

Also known as the delightfully gross-sounding *mouthfeel*, the texture of a wine is how it physically feels in your mouth. Some common descriptors are things like smooth, gritty, velvety, rich, or juicy. The texture of a wine is one of my favorite parts about a tasting because you can be as simple as saying something is "fuzzy" or go as far as "it's like licking the side of my grandmother's couch."

Tannins

Tannins are astringent biomolecules found in many plants, including grape skins, seeds, and stems, and in some wood, such as oak. That feeling like you just ate a whole box of dryer sheets when you're drinking a red wine? That comes from tannins, either from the grapes or from barrel aging. Aside from giving wine (and your mouth) a dry and puckering texture, tannins can add bitterness to a wine . . . and to dinner parties where someone will undoubtedly blame them for their "wine headaches." While tannins *can* give people headaches, whether it's as dire as your homie's dramatic new girlfriend makes it out to be is debatable. Black tea is just as strong in tannins, so if you can sip a cup of that without a problem, your headache might be due to the fact that you're drinking *too much* red wine.

Finish

The finish is the flavor and sensation a wine leaves in your mouth after you've swallowed. [Insert innuendo of choice.] They're usually talked about in terms of length, like a short, crisp finish or a long, dry finish. When you take all the qualities of a wine's taste into consideration, you can also talk about things like complexity and balance. The **complexity** refers to how dimensional a wine is. The more layers of flavors and textures, the more complex the wine. The **balance** of a wine is how well all those different flavors and textures work together. A balanced wine is seamless, with everything just in its right place.

And then, you're done! Now you just get to drink and have opinions!

. . . Unless you want to take it to the next level and finish your tasting with the Ross Test. **The Ross Test** is my highly scientific contribution to the art of wine tasting, where you judge a wine based on whether or not you can swig it straight from the bottle. Some wines are great for swigging and others aren't, and I believe that's an important thing for a wine drinker to know. We all have times we want to celebrate and we all have bad days, both occasions when you may just not have the time or willpower to find a glass. So take your bottle and throw it back a couple sips. If it's delicious, it passes. If it sucks, it fails. Please be advised that most tasting rooms do not include/encourage/allow this very important technique in their tastings, even when you are Marissa A. Ross, creator of the Ross Test.

I know what you're thinking: "Damn, that's a lot to do while drinking." I promise it only looks that way on paper. In reality, it's simply paying attention to your senses, even though it doesn't always feel so simple to do. There are plenty of times when I still can't quite put my finger on what I'm smelling or tasting. But you take another sip, stay present in your senses, and do your best to pick out the different things you're tasting. You still may not know what the hell it is, but you'll be that much better for your next glass. And the next glass after that. And the next glass after that.

Because practice makes perfect. And wine-tasting practice is the best practice since *it's just drinking wine.* You're probably practicing right now! And I have to say, I love your initiative. Keep up the good work, champ.

To-Drink List:

1. Obtain a bottle of your choice.
2. Pour yourself a glass and give yourself ten minutes with each step of wine tasting, giving the appearance a good up-down, swirling, smelling, and three (or more) sips.
3. Talk out loud about what you're seeing/smelling/tasting. This may feel silly if you're alone, but along with practicing these steps, you want to practice articulating what you're sensing in each step. This will help you feel more confident talking about tasting in groups.
4. Take notes. Writing down what you're experiencing will help imprint the method, as well as help you keep track of similarities and differences between wines you're tasting. These come in handy in conversation, as well as for contrasting and comparing wines in the future. For example, if you almost always taste tobacco in Nebbiolo, you can use that as a barometer for tasting other Nebbiolos, and use that as a talking point.
5. Remember, this isn't math. Don't worry about what you think you *should* be tasting, and let yourself see, smell, and taste whatever it is you're seeing and smelling and tasting. Have fun with it!
6. Oh, and Ross Test that shit!

CHAPTER FIVE

A Noncomprehensive Guide to the Wines You Will Encounter

There is a lot of wine out there. With more than 1,300 different varietals, that is about three times the number of *Law & Order: SVU* episodes to date. Do the casual but confident and educated wine drinkers of the world need to know them all? The short answer is no. That's like making someone intensively study and train for *Jeopardy!* to go to Sunday Night Trivia at Ye Rustic Inn. Four-pound grape dictionaries are great for when you're looking to high-dive into the deep end of wine, but not very helpful when you're looking for a quick suggestion on a medium-bodied white wine that doesn't taste like someone poured you a glass of your grandma's perfume that she's had since '74. Rather than go over the hundreds of wines you will probably never see, in this chapter I'll take you through the single varietals you're most likely to encounter.

Now that you know how to taste wine, it's important to always be trying new wines. This can sometimes be daunting, because it's easy to fall into the habit of drinking the same styles of wine. I have to constantly remind myself that there are wines in the world other than light-bodied French reds, not only because it's my job to write about all kinds of wine, but because I can't get better by drinking the same stuff over and over. The only way to keep learning, expanding your palate, and practicing different descriptors is by constantly trying wines you've never had before.

One of the perks of being my friend, aside from knowing I will always bring bomb-ass Champagne to celebrate the cool shit you've accomplished, is that you can always hit me up to ask me about a wine you've never heard of. Because even if you've found your wine shop, and you're asking questions, and you trust them, it still feels nice to ask a reliable friend who knows what's up. And what this chapter is is you texting me, asking, "Hey, what's the deal with Godello?" and getting my tasting notes texted back quicker than a desperate booty call. Use this chapter as a fast reference guide or a shopping list for new wines to try.

"Where the Hell Did She Get Violets?!"

After trying some of these wines, you may disagree with my tasting notes. And that's totally chill. Wine is a lot like love. Not only is it intoxicating, it's one of those things that no one can experience quite like you did. There are too many factors—it will never be that right time of day, with that exact song playing, with just enough cologne fading into the oils of that neck, with that exact blend of history and optimism. Those moments are impossible to truly share, and they are fleeting. Even you, the person who lived it, are left with only a memory. A recollection that can never be replicated, no matter how hard you try. Wine, like love, is unpredictable and constantly evolving. From region to region, vintage to vintage, and even bottle to bottle, your experience and mine may differ. But that's what makes wine so exciting to drink, to talk about, and to fall in love with.

RED WINES
Barbera

Medium Body / High Acidity / Low Tannins

This varietal is found primarily in Piemonte, Italy, and its wine is rich in flavor but feels light bodied because of its low tannins and high acidity. Cranberries, blackberries, cherry, and pine make it both fruity and woodsy. You know that warm, fuzzy, "I want to hug everyone!" feeling? It's that. Mixed with Christmas. Mixed with even more juicy berries.

Cabernet Franc

Medium Body / Medium-High Acidity / Medium-High Tannins

The first thing that comes to mind when I think of Cabernet Franc is bell peppers. It has some fruit on it, like cranberry, strawberry, and plum, as well as some gravelly minerality, but it is mostly known for its herbaceous spice. I liken this to cooking fajitas with someone you just started dating who's a little edgy and you're not quite sure if they even like you, but they're so snuggly!

Cabernet Sauvignon

Full Body / Medium Acidity / High Tannins

In my early years, I swore up and down that California Cab Sauv was the only wine for me. While it will always have a special place in my heart, I now reserve drinking it for decadent evenings. Its heavy body, bold dark fruit, tobacco, and pepper flavors are best served with food just as rich, rather than drinking it on an empty stomach at happy hour.

Carignan

Light-Medium Body / Medium-High Acidity / Medium Tannins

A dusty (and spicy) fruit bowl of a wine that proves you can play both sides without being an asshole. It can feel light and deserving of some space in your fridge for a summer afternoon, or it can be taken seriously at the dinner table with fall-inspired dishes (think Thanksgiving). It's fun, but has a weight to it. It reminds me of the dance scene in *Pulp Fiction*: as playful as the Swim, but it's as deep as Uma Thurman's stare.

Cinsault

Light Body / Low Acidity / Low Tannins

Cinsault is an easy drinker that flies under the radar, because it has been used primarily as a blending grape and for rosés. But much like Beyoncé, Cinsault shines when it goes solo. It may be light bodied and fruity with cranberry and strawberry, but its pepper, dash of salt, and inexplicable meaty quality makes it more savory than other light, juicy reds. I've been known to describe them as "grab-your-tits good," so do what you will with that information.

Counoise

Light Body / High Acidity / Low Tannins

This is another light red that people have buried in blends, but I say bring me a full bottle of it any day. Counoise is a Lite-Brite of tart cranberry and spiced strawberry that I love having chilled for day drinking, whether I'm in a bikini or in my sweatpants. It's rosé for those of us who would prefer a red over a rosé (please don't kill me).

Gamay

Light Body / Medium-High Acidity / Low Tannins

Gamay, with its tart red berries, black currant, and subtle floral notes of peony and violet, is the love of my wine life. I drink it almost daily and find its many iterations, from gluggy Nouveau juice to unsuspectingly bold, smooth, and nuanced crus like Moulin-à-Vent and Morgon, to be the most delicious thing on the planet. Crowd pleasing but also intimate, Gamay is basically a jukebox with at least one of everyone's favorite songs loaded up.

Grenache

Medium Body / Medium Acidity / Medium Tannins

I will admit that I have a strained relationship with Grenache. Many times its candied strawberry and raspberry flavors remind me of fruit snacks and I want nothing to do with it, although most people love it. My preferred type of Grenache is Spain's Hairy Grenache. It's related to regular Grenache and has the same bright berry notes, but with more balsamic and bitter flavors.

Lambrusco

Light to Medium Body / Medium-High Acidity / Medium Tannins

Many people write off Lambrusco because they end up with a sweet one, but traditional Lambrusco is dry and prickly. Originally made to pair with the cuisine of its region, Emilia-Romagna, Lambruscos are excellent food wines and pair well with everything from pasta to cheeseburgers. Perfect for those who love bubbles but shy from sweet, and anyone who likes to make any day a festive and celebratory occasion.

Malbec

Medium-Full Body / Medium Acidity / Medium Tannins

Malbec from Argentina is what most people think of when it comes to Malbec: rich, powerhouse of blackberries, plum, and tobacco. These are great full-bodied food wines because of their short finish and the fact that they don't overpower leaner meats. But France also does Malbec, and they call it Côt. And goddamn do I love it. Driven by minerality rather than fruit, Côt is lighter and a bit spicier, but still delivers on savory plums.

Montepulciano

Medium Body / Medium Acidity / Medium Tannins

Italy's other pizza wine aside from Sangiovese, these juicy reds always remind me of Rome. It has lively cranberry, sour cherry, and minerality that finishes smooth. It's vibrant and energetic like a crazed taxi navigating traffic around the seven hills, while somehow maintaining that classic calm and casual elegance that all Italians (even the yelling ones) seem to possess.

Mourvèdre

Full Body / Medium Acidity / High Tannins

Mourvèdre is like a big, flowery bouquet of spareribs. While I don't think I would like to have that waiting for me on my doorstep after work, I do like it in a glass. Mourvèdre is plummy and spicy, with dark berries, smoke, and, well, meat.

All these qualities make it an essential red wine for grilling and barbeque.

Nebbiolo

Medium-Full Body / High Acidity / High Tannins

Nebbiolo is like jumping into a pool that doesn't look that cold, and then you are shocked upon impact. You smell it and you're convinced it's going to be an easygoing wine, and then it punches you in the mouth with its high tannins. But in a good way! It tastes like a big red fruit that is grown in the middle of the Forbidden Forest from *Harry Potter*, but with more flowers and less scary stuff. It has a little bit of everything: bright cherry, floral notes of roses and violets, and wet clay.

Nero d'Avola

Full Body / Medium-High Acidity / Medium-High Tannins

Nero d'Avola is a dusty European cowboy covered in jam. Riding in from a nonexistent desert on the outskirts of Italy that I have dreamed up, Nero is blackberry and plum jam, with hints of smoke, tobacco, and a bit of spice.

Pineau d'Aunis

Light Body / High Acidity / Low Tannins

Pineau d'Aunis is like Gamay's cousin that is in a very indie band that no one really knows about but you do, and by God, you're going to let people know that you love their self-released EP. Basically, this is the wine that gets me called a hipster the most. It's primarily been used in blends over the years, but now the grape that is just as bright, tart, and chuggable as Gamay is getting some shelf time, too. It's one of my favorite "writing wines," meaning I can drink it like water.

Pinot Noir

Light Body / Medium-High Acidity / Medium-Low Tannins

The thin-skinned grape that came to the fore in *Sideways* is my idea of a fuzzy throw blanket of a wine. It's light but warm, with bright cranberry, raspberry, and cherry notes, and a lingering finish that you could curl up in. And it can go anywhere! Throw blankets are for the living room, for the bed, for picnics, and same goes for Pinot Noir. It's versatile as hell, and I've yet to find anyone to turn one down while hanging out on the couch.

Sangiovese

Light-Medium Body / High Acidity / High Tannins

The patron saint of Italian wine (well, at least in my religion), Sangiovese is as diverse as Italy's cuisine. There's lighter, fruit-forward Sangiovese that you can throw back like paper-thin margherita pizza, and there's rustic, tannic Sangiovese that feels more like a hearty Bolognese. Either way, you'll encounter flavors of tart cherry and tomato. And if you don't see any straight-up Sangiovese, grab yourself some Chianti, which is also made of Sangiovese grapes. You might recognize them from their weaved basket bases, called a fiasco bottle.

St. Laurent

Light Body / Medium-High Acidity / Medium-Low Tannins
This lesser-known Austrian grape is Pinot Noir's younger sister that dabbled in going Goth. In other words, they are in the same grape family, but there are some key differences. Like many siblings, they are undeniably related, sharing similar red fruit characteristics and structure, but St. Laurent is darker and a bit tougher, with dry, earthy notes.

Syrah

Full Body / Medium Acidity / Medium Tannins
While some Syrahs can be way over the top, a well-made Syrah is a spiritual and transformative wine, like one of those summers you come out of feeling more mature and self-assured. Bold and forward fruits like blackberry and blueberry come on strong, and taper off to a spicy and smoky finish, like the plume of a campfire drifting quietly into the night sky.

Trollinger/Schiava

Light Body / Medium Acidity / Low Tannins
Depending on whether you're in Germany or Italy, this wine may be called Trollinger or Schiava. Either way, I call it California Summer But I Wish It Was Fall wine. It's light enough to drink when it's still hot out through October, with soft strawberry and floral notes, but it has a woodsy, tobacco taste that will tide you over until fall actually arrives.

Trousseau

Light-Medium Body / Medium Acidity / Medium-High Tannins
Trousseau reminds me of a strong female lead that no one takes seriously at first because she looks delicate and likes the color pink, but once you get to know her, she turns out to be a badass. Trousseau's pale red hue may have you thinking it won't be able to hold its own, but its tannic structure is strong as hell. A gravelly babe of smoked, dried roses, Trousseau is a little bitter and not to be underestimated.

Valdiguié

Light Body / Medium Acidity / Low Tannins
Once called Napa Gamay, Valdiguié was one of the most popular grapes grown in California until Cabernet had to come and fuck it all up. Valdiguié is a very juicy, easygoing wine, with an airy floral bouquet and a palate bursting with strawberry and velvety blackberry notes. If a wine came in a juice box, this would be it.

Zinfandel

Light Body / High Acidity / Medium Tannins
Zinfandel got a bad rap in the nineties when the focus became to push the wine's ABV up past 16 percent, creating overripe, jammy wines that were just gross. While classical Zinfandel, which is, thankfully, making a comeback, is still bold with black berries and a smoky finish, it's light on its feet—and it won't get you totally wasted with crazy ABV percentages.

Zweigelt

Light Body / Medium Acidity / Low Tannins

Unfussy and youthful, Zweigelt is right up there with Gamay when it comes to being the party animals of the red varietals. Often found in crown-capped liter bottles, Austria's Zweigelt is all fresh and bright sour cherry flavor with hints of earthiness and bitter herbal notes. But not too much. Zweigelt is less for pondering over wine's complexities, and more for enjoying the hell out of.

WHITE WINES
Albariño

Light Body / High Acidity / Bone Dry

Taking a whiff of Albariño, one of the most floral white wines, whisks you away to a blossoming citrus orchard. With its mouthwatering acidity, bright lemon and lime flavors, and elevated minerality, this Spanish wine reminds me of sipping fresh limeade on a springtime patio.

Assyrtiko

Medium-Full Body / High Acidity / Dry

If you've been dying to holiday in Santorini but can only afford a bottle of wine, Assyrtiko is the one for you. This Greek wine from Santorini is poppy and fun, but elegant and smooth. It will make you feel as if you're traipsing along the isle's famous white-structured skylines with waves of crisp citrus, apple, and high minerality crashing upon your taste buds.

Chablis

Light-Medium Body / High Acidity / Bone Dry
Don't let grocery store box wine, which co-opted the name, scare you away from Chablis. The Chardonnay for those who cringe over robust California Chardonnays, Burgundy's Chablis is 100 percent Chardonnay, unoaked, lean and zesty with steely citrus, limestone, and a touch of seawater. It's sophisticated as hell, and treasured by wine enthusiasts around the world for its minerality.

Chardonnay

Medium-Full Body / Medium Acidity / Dry
Chardonnay heavily takes on the characteristics of its fermentation. If you're into buttery, vanilla-y Chardonnays, get yourself an oaked Chardonnay. Personally, I think oak is often an asshole who is trying to steal Chardonnay's spotlight. With neutral fermentations like steel or concrete, Chardonnay's fruit profile of lighter citrus, pears, and apple blossoms, or tropical notes like pineapple and passion fruit, shine with more acidity and nods to terroir.

Chenin Blanc

Light Body / Medium-High Acidity / Dry–Off-Dry

I'm not one for astrology, but Chenin Blanc is a bit of a Gemini. It can be dry or it can be sweet, and depending on your taste, you should talk to your wine shop to make sure you're getting what you want. (Hint: If you see SEC on the label, it's dry.) Because of its high acidity, it tastes great either way, with notes of soft apples, pears, orange marmalade, and honey.

Gewürztraminer

Light Body / Medium-Low Acidity / Semi-Sweet

Gewürztraminer always reminds me of a Polynesian sweet and sour sauce. Strikingly aromatic with heavy tropical notes of lychee and flower leis, it tastes like pineapple, orange, and savory brown sugar. It's one of the toughest wines in regular rotation to pronounce, but don't worry. Every time I say this word, I sound like a character speaking backward in Agent Cooper's dream sequence from *Twin Peaks*, so you're not alone.

Grüner Veltliner

Light Body / High Acidity / Dry

Grüner is very green. Its bottles are dark green, the wine itself is a pale yellow green, and it smells like a farmers' market haul of green beans, herbs, and citrus. The good news is, drinking it is less like finishing your vegetables and more like drinking crisp green apple and lime with Pop Rocks.

Muscadet/Melon de Bourgogne

Light Body / High Acidity / Bone Dry

If I was in marketing, my slogan for this wine would be: "Need a beach day? Sail away with a bottle of Muscadet!" Muscadet (also known as Melon de Bourgogne) is driven by minerality, and tastes like sipping on a salted cantaloupe slushie with fresh-squeezed limes while watching waves crash upon the shore.

Pinot Grigio/Pinot Gris

Light-Medium Body / Medium-High Acidity / Dry

Pinot Grigio is what Italians call it, and Pinot Gris is what the French call it, but it's the same damn grape. Pinot G is one of the all-time champion day-drinking wines. Fresh and zippy, it smells like citrus and honeysuckle, and tastes like you just sat back in a lawn chair in your backyard with some homegrown lemons, limes, and not quite ripe white peach.

Riesling

Light Body / High Acidity / Dry–Off-Dry

One of the wine world's most beloved grapes, there is a Riesling for everyone. Depending on the region, Riesling ranges from tasting like a juicy pack of Starbursts to grapefruits dusted with granular sugar. No matter how dry you go, Riesling is peachy and floral, and will pair with whatever you're eating.

Sauvignon Blanc

Light-Medium Body / High Acidity / Dry

Sauvignon Blanc tastes just like it looks: sunny. It reminds me of a glass of spring on the cusp of summer. It has the spongy innards of Meyer lemon, lime, wet grass, and a little hot concrete. Maybe even a faint sea breeze.

Sémillon

Full Body / Medium Acidity / Dry

Sémillon is like Chardonnay and Sauvignon Blanc's love child. Both rich and refreshing, on the nose it's like lemon meringue pie with a little spice on the crust. Its body and texture are reminiscent of Chardonnay, full and waxy, while its palate is more Sauv Blanc with tangy apple, lemon, and candied ginger.

Txakoli

Light Body / High Acidity / Bone Dry

It may be one of the hardest wines to pronounce, but *Cha-co-lee* is one of the easiest wines to throw back. Airy, effervescent, and salty, Spain's Txakoli is as irresistible as a bowl of potato chips. Its clean-cut citrus and brisk white flowers coupled with a heightened acidity and minerality make it zingy, refreshing, and impossible to keep your hands off of.

Vermentino

Light Body / Medium-High Acidity / Dry

Primarily grown on the Italian island of Sardinia, Vermentino is a Mediterranean daydream. It smells and tastes like a picnic of pears and pink grapefruits dusted with sea salt on a white pebbled beach. It is Gwyneth Paltrow and Jude Law smiling in the surf of an Italian beach in *The Talented Mr. Ripley*—youthful, idyllic, and summery.

Vinho Verde

Light Body / High Acidity / Dry

The LaCroix of wine. Portugal's Vinho Verde is lightly effervescent, goes down like water, and is addictive. It tastes like grapefruit lemonade, with hints of melon and Paul McCartney's sweat. No, I have not licked Paul McCartney, but if I did, I bet it would be crisp, salty, and intoxicating and I would drink bottles of it. Cherry on top: It's superaffordable, usually around ten bucks a bottle.

Viognier

Full Body / Low-Medium Acidity / Dry

Viognier smells like a perfume you actually want to drink, with aromas not unlike a favorite Bath & Body Works scent. Yes, it's strong, but you love it. The bouquet smells like an actual bouquet of peach blossoms and honeysuckle, but the palate is a thick, cool wind of tropical fruits à la mode.

ROSÉ WINES
Cabernet Franc

Light Body / High Acidity / Dry

Dry but refreshing, Cabernet Franc rosé is a welcome summer breeze, wafting in rose hips and limestone minerality. It tastes just as summery as it smells, with notes of raspberry, cucumber, and that beachy hair spray that smells like the ocean, but better.

Gamay

Light Body / High Acidity / Dry

Sassy and tart, Gamay rosé lives up to its fuller red counterparts. On the nose, you have raspberry Lemonheads, white flowers, and hints of pink grapefruit. The palate is like chilled strawberries dipped in a Ziploc baggy of half Himalayan sea salt and half the powder found at the bottom of a Sour Patch Kids box.

Grenache

Medium Body / Medium Acidity / Dry

Grenache rosé is more mature than other rosés. Savory and supple, the nose is exuberant with rhubarb, anise, and red fruits, and it tastes like maraschino cherries draped in velvet. Grenache rosé prefers dinner to day drinking, as it pairs fabulously with food. It reminds me of Padma Lakshmi: always elegant, and very fun after a glass or two.

Pinot Noir

Light Body / Medium-High Acidity / Dry

Lighthearted but sentimental, Pinot Noir rosé subtly tiptoes in from a wet garden and down a hall of strawberry and watermelon into your bed. It's fruity, earthy, sexy, with a good laugh—like an acoustic but upbeat Father John Misty jam.

Provençal Rosé

Light Body / Medium Acidity / Dry

This is the only blend I'm covering because it would be too insane for me to try to cover all the blends, but this is a must. Generally, when you're "looking for rosé," this is the wine that comes to mind. These varying blends of Grenache, Cinsault, Syrah, and Mourvèdre are lean and fruity with strawberry and watermelon, with a slightly salty finish. There wouldn't be a rosé season without 'em.

Syrah

Light-Medium Body / High Acidity / Dry

One of those electropop songs kept in rhythm by a strong beat. It smells and tastes like neon strawberry and orange zest with firecracker acidity that could break free into a rager of sharp red fruits, but with enough textural structure to keep it together.

ORANGE WINES

Refresher! Orange wines are white wines that are made like red wines. That's also going to be the name of my Dr. Seuss–style picture book for adults.

Chardonnay

Medium Body / Medium Acidity / Dry

If someone made a soft shag rug out of lemon zest, apples, and honey, that's what drinking skin-fermented Chardonnay tastes like. It's plush, it's sultry, and it leaves you wondering why you spent so many years shaming Chardonnay, because now it's all you want to get down on.

Godello

Medium Body / Medium-High Acidity / Dry

Drinking an orange Godello feels like you're draping your mouth in the finest fabric of Spain. It smells like rich Golden Delicious apples drenched in maple syrup, tastes like silk crepe strewn out of lemon-pineapple SweeTarts, and feels like you're going to drink the whole bottle and need a siesta.

Macabeo/Viura

Medium Body / High Acidity / Dry

The orange wine for people who've never had orange wine. It's funky for sure, but it's also approachable. Strong aromatics of honey, dried flowers, and peaches give way to a similar palate that is taut with acidity, textural but smooth, leaving an overall feeling like it's waltzing through your mouth rather than stomping around.

Pinot Gris

Medium Body / Medium Acidity / Dry

Pinot Gris smells like mandarins, pears, and spiced saltwater taffy. The color is vibrant and almost coral, and the palate is just as punchy as it looks, with notes of bright citrus, pears, and apples.

SPARKLING WINES
Cava

Light Body / High Acidity / Dry

Cava is one of those things that seems too good to be true, but it *is* true and it is indeed very good. A blend of Macabeo, Xarel-lo, and Parellada, Cava is made just like Champagne but with a Vinho Verde price tag. The Spanish sparkler bursts with bright lemongrass, green apples, and fine scrubby bubbles, and it makes celebrating (even on ordinary days) affordable.

Champagne

Light to Full Body / Medium to High Acidity / Off-Dry to Dry
Champagne varies depending on how dry you're going and
how old it is, but who are we kidding? It's fucking Champagne!
The muse of rappers, yacht owners, and normal people everywhere, Champagne is revered for its delicate but structured
bubbles and elegance. Most widely made with Chardonnay,
Pinot Noir, and Pinot Meunier, it's a delicious splurge with
notes of lemon, gardenia, and nutty pastry.

Crémant

Light Body / Medium-High Acidity / Dry
You don't need to understand French to know the word *Crémant* means "chill bubbles." Made in méthode traditionnelle
like Champagne but at a lower atmospheric pressure, Crémant drinks like a white wine but still feels like a party. These
wines' flavor varies from AOC to AOC, like Crémant d'Alsace
and Crémant de Loire, but they are extremely light on the
nose, and the palate is effortless and scrumptious, with notes
of crisp apples, pears, and my mother's lemon bars.

Franciacorta

Light to Full Body / High Acidity / Dry
The middle sister between Champagne and Cava in the fairy tale
of sparkling wines is Franciacorta. This méthode traditionnelle
Italian wine is fruity and floral with notes of apricot, lemon, and
almonds. When aged, it can become creamy like Champagne.

Pétillant Naturel

Light-Medium Body / High Acidity / Dry

Remember the sparkling wines that get capped before they're done fermenting? These are the ones! Because they can be made with any grape, their flavor profiles are all over the place, but they are almost always unfiltered and are always, always fun. Tart, lively, with a taste reminiscent of kombucha, these are some of my all-time favorite wines.

Prosecco

Light-Medium Body / Medium Acidity / Dry

Prosecco is the sundress of sparkling wine, sweet and playful. Its youthful, floral nature comes from its tank fermentation, which preserves the wine's freshness and aromatics. On the palate, it is fruit-forward with creamy honeydew and apples.

What the Hell Is a Demi-Sec?!: Decoding Dry to Sweet

Anyone who has ever quickly run into the store for mimosa rations has probably experienced the disappointment of getting home and popping a bottle of sparkling wine you swore was the one you loved, only to find it *wayyy* sweeter. That's because the sweetness of sparkling wines varies, even if they are the same type of wine. Get exactly what you want for brunch by reading the label and looking out for these key terms.

Brut Nature: Driest, Atacama Desert dry
Extra Brut: Dry as hell
Brut: Dry
Extra Dry/Extra Sec: Pretty dry, with a tinge of sweet
Dry/Sec: Oh, shit, getting sweet
Demi-Sec: Pretty damn sweet
Doux: SO FUCKIN' SWEET

I hope this is a chapter you can always turn to, something you can open up any night of the week and never feel at a loss for what to drink. I hope it inspires you to always be trying new wines. Even after you've drank all my suggestions, I hope it inspires you to seek out the hundreds of wines I didn't list. I hope it inspires you to taste them, to describe them, to talk about them. Because you never know when you'll become the friend everyone texts from the wine shop.

You may laugh now, but if this book proves anything, it is that we are all capable of being that friend.

To-Drink List:

1. Pick a wine I've suggested to try.
2. Taste it, and record your findings either on your phone

on a wine app like Delectable or your notepad app, or get analog with it and use an actual notepad.

3. Compare and contrast against my tasting notes.

4. Think of a friend who would like that wine, and tell them all about it. Everyone loves hearing about wines they should try—it makes people feel special, and it helps you practice describing wine. Maybe even set a date to drink it together.

5. Next time you drink that wine, pick one from a different region to compare and contrast against my tasting notes and *your* tasting notes.

RED WINES

BONE DRY

DRY

GREEN

BONE DRY	DRY
BARBERA	CABERNET FRANC
COOL-CLIMATE MALBEC	COOL-CLIMATE CABERNET SAUVIGNON
MONTEPULCIANO	SANGIOVESE
NEBBIOLO	

WHITE WINES

BONE DRY

DRY

TART

BONE DRY	DRY
ALBARIÑO	ASSYRTIKO
CHABLIS	COOL-CLIMATE CHARDONNAY
MUSCADET/MELON	CHENIN BLANC
TXAKOLI	GRÜNER VELTLINER
VINHO VERDE	PINOT GRIGIO
	SAUVIGNON BLANC
	VERMENTINO

DRY

TART FRUITS

CINSAULT

COUNOISE

GAMAY

PINEAU D'AUNIS

COOL-CLIMATE
PINOT NOIR

TROLLINGER/SCHIAVA

VALDIGUIÉ

ZWEIGELT

DRY

RIPE FRUITS

CARIGNAN

GRENACHE

WARM-CLIMATE MALBEC

MOURVÈDRE

NERO D'AVOLA

WARM-CLIMATE
PINOT NOIR

ST. LAURENT

SYRAH

TROUSSEAU

ZINFANDEL

SEMI-SWEET

LAMBRUSCO

DRY

RIPE

WARM-CLIMATE
CHARDONNAY

TROCKEN RIESLING

HALBTROCKEN RIESLING

SEMILLON

SPÄTLESE RIESLING

SEMI-SWEET

PEACH, FLOWERS, &
SWEET LEMON

GEWÜRZTRAMINER

CHAPTER SIX

Regions to Recognize

Wine can be made all over the place, but there are currently ten major wine regions in the world. From Old World regions that have been making wine for thousands of years to New World regions that are just getting started, in this chapter we will take some quick trips to the top producing countries. We'll go over each region's top varietals, as well as get you thinking about terroir by exploring their soils. There won't be a geography quiz at the end of the week, but getting a grasp on the lay of the lands is essential to knowing and understanding what the hell you're drinking.

A good wine is a mirror to the land where its grapes were grown, reflective of the soil, the climate, and indigenous (or not) vegetation surrounding the vineyard. These environmental factors are what make up the fancy French word I pronounce correctly one-third of the time, *terroir* (tare-wah).

Terroir is the unique character of the land, and it plays just as big of a part in influencing the taste of wine as the grapes themselves. From the volcanic ground of Mount Etna to the cool, marine layers of the California coast, it's the natural elements of the vineyards that make each region's wines taste different, even if they are the same varietal.

Take Grenache for example. This red wine is produced all over the world and can taste like a pouch of liquefied fruit snacks or a spicy berry licorice, all depending on where it is grown. A Garnacha (aka Grenache) from the south of Spain is higher in alcohol content (ABV) and sugar because the climate is much warmer than the cool climates of the south of France where a Grenache is grown. Similarly, you can taste differences with Gamay depending on where it is grown. The granite soils of Beaujolais have a different effect on the wine than the limestone of the Loire Valley.

Cool Climate Wines vs. Warm Climate Wines

Knowing a wine's climate is a quick way to identify its characteristics. *Cool climates produce wines that are more tart and acidic. Warm climates produce wines that are riper, with more sugar and less acidity.* Chardonnay is a great example: A Chardonnay from the cool Sonoma coast will be more citrusy and acidic, while a Chardonnay from the warmer Napa clime will be more tropical, with less acidity.

Wine regions are respected in the same way many producers are, renowned for the quality and characteristics they bring to a wine. It's the difference between buying a generic leather bag from H&M and buying a soft, handcrafted Italian leather bag. Many countries have government-sanctioned designations and certifications so that you aren't being sold a bunch of swill labeled as Champagne when it's grown in Chino Hills, California. You may recognize acronyms such as AOP, AOC, or DOC, all respectfully meaning "Yo, this shit is legit!" These designations are regulated with strict codes that specify how wines can be made, what grapes can be used, and even how long the wine can be aged in certain regions. While these designations do give credit to the validity of a wine's region, they don't necessarily mean the wine is awesome. A winemaker can play by the rules and still make bad wine, just like a winemaker can throw middle fingers at the rules, not get certified, and still make delicious wine. Think of it more like Oprah's Book Club—trustworthy, but not the only indicator of a good read.

The sheer number of regions is daunting, but you don't need to worry about knowing each and every one. If memorizing the names of plots of land was a requirement to enjoy and know about wine, I would not be here today. It's just important to start thinking about regions and terroir, and their effect on wine and their effect on what wines you like (or don't). Take a second with each wine and register where it is from while you're drinking it. Even if you have no idea where that place is, still take a moment to put it in your brain. You don't need to have visited Tuscany to think to yourself, "All right, Tuscany, Italy, got it," and imagine a faraway villa on a sunlit hillside, perhaps with Diane Lane on the balcony, and a pool of *cacio e pepe*.* The more wine you drink, the more familiar you will become with regions. No need for flash cards, because when you find a region you love, you will have a literal thirst for knowledge.

Now let's get to jet-setting. We have two leisurely legs to our trip: Old World and New World. Get cozy with these terms because they are used in two different ways in the wine world. Not only can they be used to reference physical locations, but they can also be used as descriptors. Both Old World and New World relate to specific styles of wine traditional for that area, but it's not like you can't make an Old World–style wine in a New World region.

Old World wines are from countries that have been making wine for thousands of years, such as France, Germany, Italy, Portugal, and Spain. These wines are lighter in body, higher in acidity, and lower in alcohol.

---

* I have been to Tuscany and, sadly, did not see any Diane Lanes *or* pools of pasta. But that's not what's important. What's important is making a mental note, however you need to.

FRANCE

CHAMPAGNE

ALSACE

LOIRE

BOURGOGNE

JURA

BEAUJOLAIS

BORDEAUX

RHÔNE

PROVENCE

LANGUEDOC-
ROUSSILLON

From the bare necessities of life to its most decadent luxuries, the French are always elemental but elegant. It's no surprise that this is where the notion of terroir really took off, because the French value simplicity over convolution. This minimalism and respect for the land produces timeless wines that are as casual as a striped T-shirt and as sumptuous as quilted Chanel. Drinking French wines is a lesson in subtle style and sophistication, whether you're enjoying a blend from a tiny village or a revered red off the auction block of Sotheby's. Here are some of the most recognized regions you'll find in France.

Alsace

Northeast France

THE GIST: Dry, aromatic, and fruit-forward white wines that are heavily inspired by their German neighbors

SOIL TYPES: Clay, granite, limestone, sandstone, volcanic rock

MAIN VARIETALS: Gewürztraminer, Pinot Blanc, Pinot Gris, Muscat, Riesling, and Sylvaner

Get a Cru

Within many of France's regions and subregions, there are also crus. *A cru is a specific vineyard or group of vineyards, usually recognized for its distinctive terroir and/or the wine's unique characteristics.* Moulin-à-Vent, for example, is revered for its soil of pink granite and magnesium, with wines that are the most structured and robust from Beaujolais. France also uses the terms *premier cru* and *grand cru* to indicate wines from individual villages or prized vineyards.

Beaujolais

East Central France

THE GIST: Light, tart, glou-glou reds

SOIL TYPES: Granite, limestone, sandstone

CRUS/SUBREGIONS TO GET ACQUAINTED WITH: Brouilly, Chiroubles, Fleurie, Juliénas, Morgon, Moulin-à-Vent, Régnié, Saint-Amour

Bordeaux

Western France

THE GIST: Elegant, medium-bodied blends

SOIL TYPES: Bordeaux is divided into two banks; the left bank is known for gravel soils and the right bank is known for clay and limestone.

SUBREGIONS TO GET ACQUAINTED WITH:

> **LEFT BANK:** Margaux, Médoc, Pauillac, Saint-Estèphe, Saint-Julien

> **RIGHT BANK:** Canon-Fronsac, Côtes-de-Blaye, Côtes-de-Bourg, Fronsac, Pomerol, Saint-Émilion

MAIN VARIETALS: Cabernet Franc, Cabernet Sauvignon, Merlot, Malbec, Petit Verdot, Sauvignon Blanc, Sémillon

Burgundy (or, as It Is Known in France, Bourgogne)

East Central France

THE GIST: The gold standard of Pinot Noir and Chardonnay

SOIL TYPES: Limestone, chalk

SUBREGIONS TO GET ACQUAINTED WITH: Chablis, Côte de Beaune, Côte Chalonnaise, Côte de Nuits, Mâconnais

MAIN VARIETALS: Chardonnay, Pinot Noir

Champagne

Northern France

THE GIST: The best of the bubbles

SOIL TYPES: Limestone, chalk

SUBREGIONS TO GET ACQUAINTED WITH: Côte des Blancs, Côte de Sézanne, Montagne de Reims, Vallée de la Marne, the Aube

MAIN VARIETALS: Chardonnay, Pinot Noir

Côtes du Rhône

Southeast France

THE GIST: Wide range, from savory and sexy to light and approachable

SOIL TYPES: Clay, granite, limestone, sand

SUBREGIONS TO GET ACQUAINTED WITH:

> **NORTHERN RHÔNE:** Condrieu, Cornas, Côte-Rôtie, Crozes-Hermitage, Hermitage, Saint-Joseph, Saint-Péray

> **SOUTHERN RHÔNE:** Beaumes de Venise, Châteauneuf-du-Pape, Lirac, Rasteau, Tavel, Vacqueyras, Vinsobres

MAIN VARIETALS: Cinsault, Counoise, Grenache Noir, Marsanne, Roussanne, Syrah, Ugni Blanc, Viognier

Jura

Eastern France

THE GIST: Out there, oxidized white wines

SOIL TYPE: Gravel

SUBREGIONS TO GET ACQUAINTED WITH: Arbois, Château-Chalon, Côtes du Jura, Crémant du Jura, L'Étoile, Macvin du Jura

MAIN VARIETALS: Chardonnay, Pinot Noir, Trousseau

Languedoc-Roussillon

Southern France

THE GIST: Subtle, rustic reds

SOIL TYPES: Chalk, gravel, limestone, sand, silt

SUBREGIONS TO GET ACQUAINTED WITH: Corbières, Coteaux du Languedoc, Faugères, Minervois, Saint-Chinian

MAIN VARIETALS: Cabernet Sauvignon, Chardonnay, Merlot, Sauvignon Blanc, Syrah, Viognier

Loire

Western France

THE GIST: Lots of acid

SOIL TYPES: Granite, gravel, limestone, volcanic rock

SUBREGIONS TO GET ACQUAINTED WITH: Bourgueil, Chinon, Crémant de Loire, Montlouis, Muscadet, Pouilly-Fumé, Sancerre, Touraine, Vouvray

MAIN VARIETALS: Cabernet Franc, Chardonnay, Chenin Blanc, Côt, Gamay, Grolleau, Pineau d'Aunis, Pinot Noir, Sauvignon Blanc

Provence

Southeast France

THE GIST: Rosé all day

SOIL TYPES: Clay, limestone, sandstone, shale

SUBREGIONS TO GET ACQUAINTED WITH: Bandol, Coteaux d'Aix-en-Provence, Les Baux-de-Provence

MAIN VARIETALS: Cabernet Sauvignon, Chardonnay, Grenache, Marsanne, Mourvèdre, Viognier, Sauvignon Blanc, Sémillon, Syrah

GERMANY

From their prolific Rieslings to the fresh Müller-Thurgau, Germany's white wines are some of the most revered in the world, with their fruit-forward palate and dynamic acidity. But their reds, like the mouthful Spätburgunder (Pinot Noir) and Dornfelder are just as fresh and lively due to the cool German climates. While you may have trouble pronouncing anything on a German label, you won't have any problems drinking what's in the bottle.

Don't Fear the Riesling

People hear "Riesling," immediately gasp, and go on a rant about how all Rieslings are sweet. Not true! Rieslings are also dry. *Look for trocken Rieslings for bone dry, and halbtrocken Rieslings for dry.*

Mosel-Saar-Ruwer

West Central Germany

THE GIST: Racy Rieslings from Germany's coolest climate
SOIL TYPES: Slate
MAIN VARIETALS: Müller-Thurgau, Riesling

Pfalz

Southwest Germany

THE GIST: Warmer-climate dry wines from varied varietals
SOIL TYPES: Calcareous, sandstone, basalt, volcanic
MAIN VARIETALS: Dornfelder, Müller-Thurgau, Riesling

Rheingau

Central Germany

THE GIST: Fruit-forward wines with pronounced minerality
SOIL TYPES: Marl, slate, sand
MAIN VARIETALS: Riesling, Spätburgunder (Pinot Noir)

ITALY

Italy feels like home. It's in the people and in the food, rustic and loud with big hugs and red sauces. This sentiment also comes standard in their wine. Because in Italy, wine is just like family and food: an integral part of daily life that is served out of both love and necessity. When drinking Italian wines, remember that they are generally made to complement the region's cuisine, because Italians do not separate wine as a beverage as much as they include it as a part of a meal. Whether it's with dinner with loved ones or an aperitif with your cat, you can always count on Italian wines to leave your heart as full as a big bowl of bucatini.

Abruzzo

Central Southern Italy

THE GIST: Rich, herbaceous reds

SOIL TYPES: Clay, stone

MAIN VARIETALS: Montepulciano, Sangiovese, Trebbiano

Friuli-Venezia Giulia

Northeast Italy

THE GIST: Sexy, energized white wines

SOIL TYPES: Clay, gravel, sand, sandstone

MAIN VARIETALS: Cabernet Franc, Cabernet Sauvignon, Chardonnay, Merlot, Pinot Grigio, Ribolla Gialla, Sauvignon Blanc

Piemonte

Northwest Italy

THE GIST: The place for powerful, poignant Nebbiolo

SOIL TYPES: Clay, limestone, sand

SUBREGION TO GET ACQUAINTED WITH: Asti

MAIN VARIETALS: Arneis, Barbera, Barolo, Cortese, Dolcetto, Moscato, Nebbiolo

Sardegna

Western Island

THE GIST: Salty white wines that taste like vacation in a bottle

SOIL TYPES: Granite, limestone, sandstone

MAIN VARIETALS: Cabernet Sauvignon, Cannonau (Grenache), Carignan, Malvasia, Moscato, Vermentino

Sicilia

Southern Island

THE GIST: Dark, fruit-forward reds and oceanic whites

SOIL TYPES: Sand, rock, volcanic rock

MAIN VARIETALS: Catarratto, Grillo, Inzolia, Nero d'Avola

Trentino-Alto Adige

Northern Italy

THE GIST: Austrian wines with Italian sharpness and spice

SOIL TYPE: Gravel

MAIN VARIETALS: Pinot Blanc, Pinot Grigio, Gewürztraminer, Müller-Thurgau, Schiava

Tuscany

Central Italy

THE GIST: Home of Chianti

SOIL TYPES: Sand, rock

MAIN VARIETALS: Cabernet Sauvignon, Chardonnay, Merlot, Montepulciano, Sangiovese, Sauvignon Blanc, Trebbiano

Umbria

Central Italy

THE GIST: Fruity reds and minerally whites

SOIL TYPES: Clay, limestone, volcanic rock

MAIN VARIETALS: Grechetto, Sagrantino, Sangiovese, Trebbiano

Veneto

Northeast Italy

THE GIST: Great red blends, and the white wine Soave

SOIL TYPES: Clay, gravel, sand, volcanic rock

MAIN VARIETALS: Cabernet Sauvignon, Chardonnay, Corvina, Merlot, Pinot Grigio, Prosecco, Rondinella, Trebbiano

PORTUGAL

Portugal isn't just for port. Portugal is also home to the refreshing, effervescent white wine Vinho Verde and dry reds from the Douro region.

SOIL TYPES: Sand, limestone

MAIN VARIETALS: Alvarinho, Arinto, Baga, Loureiro, Tempranillo (known as Tinta Roriz or Aragonez), Touriga Franca, Touriga Nacional

AUSTRIA

Though it may seem like Austria makes wine much like its neighbor Germany, Austria is actually warmer. Most famous for the crisp white Grüner Veltliner, Austria also produces some of the finest dry, full-bodied whites.

SOIL TYPES: Alluvial, granite, gneiss, loess, limestone, slate

MAIN VARIETALS: Blaufränkisch, Grüner Veltliner, Pinot Blanc, Pinot Noir, Riesling, Welschriesling, Zweigelt

GREECE

Greek wines are much like its landscape: refreshing but volatile, like a cold ocean mist after a wave crashes on a volcanic beach. The diverse climates of Greece, ranging from warm and Mediterranean to cool and coastal, allow for both rich, tannic reds like Xynomavro and briny whites like Assyrtiko.

SOIL TYPES: Limestone, volcanic, loam, clay, schist, marl

MAIN VARIETALS: Agiorgitiko, Assyrtiko, Mandilaria, Roditis, Xynomavro

SPAIN

When I think of Spain, I think of its rugged terrain and its rich food. Their wines are reflective of both of these things, both highly textural and opulent, like biting into a croquette with a gravelly coat and a velvety center. They're rough around the edges, but in a good way. As Spanish cuisine begins to move from paellas and toward lighter, modern dishes, you will find their wines adapting as well.

Penedès

Northeast Spain

THE GIST: Cava, cava, cava! And heavy-hitting reds

SOIL TYPES: Gravel, sand, silt

MAIN VARIETALS: Chardonnay, Garnacha, Macabeo, Merlot, Monastrell (Mourvèdre), Parellada, Xarel-lo (all of which can be used for Cava as well as single varietal white wines), Tempranillo

Priorat

Northeast Spain

THE GIST: Massive red wines

SOIL TYPES: Rock, slate

MAIN VARIETALS: Cabernet Sauvignon, Garnacha, Merlot, Tempranillo

Rías Baixas

Northwest Spain

THE GIST: Aromatic white wines

SOIL TYPES: Granite, sand, clay

MAIN VARIETAL: Albariño

Ribera del Duero

Central Spain

THE GIST: Flinty, rich, and vibrant red wines

SOIL TYPES: Sand, limestone, gravel

MAIN VARIETALS: Cabernet Sauvignon, Garnacha, Tempranillo, Tinto Fino

Rioja

Northern Central Spain

THE GIST: Renowned Tempranillos

SOIL TYPES: Clay, limestone, sandstone

MAIN VARIETALS: Garnacha, Macabeo (Viura), Tempranillo

Rueda

Northern Central Spain

THE GIST: Herbaceous but juicy white wines

SOIL TYPES: Gravel, stone, limestone

MAIN VARIETALS: Verdejo

New World wines are from countries that have only recently gotten into the wine game, like Argentina, Australia, and the US. These wines are ripe, fruity, and high in alcohol.

ARGENTINA

If you haven't had much Argentinian wine, you're not alone. Despite being one of the most prolific wine-producing countries in the world, up until recently, most of Argentina's wines were primarily consumed by the Argentinians themselves. But with the explosive success of their Malbec, which has now taken precedence over the French version of the varietal, Argentina has begun to export more of their rustic, ripe wines. With everything from velvety reds to aromatic and floral whites, Argentina has something for everyone and so much to explore.

La Rioja

Northern Argentina

THE GIST: Argentina's oldest wine region, known for Torrontés

SOIL TYPES: Clay, silt

MAIN VARIETALS: Syrah, Torrontés

Mendoza

Central Western Argentina

THE GIST: This is where your favorite Malbec is from.

SOIL TYPES: Sand, silt, clay

MAIN VARIETALS: Cabernet Sauvignon, Cereza, Chardonnay, Criolla Grande, Malbec, Tempranillo

Patagonia

Southern Argentina

THE GIST: Crisp and carbonite reds from Argentina's coolest region

SOIL TYPES: Alluvial, stones, gravel, limestone

MAIN VARIETALS: Malbec, Merlot, Pinot Noir

Salta

Northwest Argentina

THE GIST: Full-bodied reds grown amongst red-rock formations

SOIL TYPES: Sand, clay

MAIN VARIETALS: Cabernet Sauvignon, Malbec, Merlot, Tannat

AUSTRALIA

Australia may be best known for their jammy and full-bodied reds, but the warm-climate continent down under has more to offer than the cheap and sweet wines with furry outback friends on the label. Much like California, Australia is starting to experiment in their cooler climates, making more delicate wines that are closer in resemblance to French Syrah than grocery store Shiraz.

New South Wales

Southeast Australia

THE GIST: Divine aged Sémillons

SOIL TYPES: Loam, clay, sandstone

MAIN VARIETALS: Chardonnay, Sémillon, Shiraz, Tempranillo, Verdelho

South Australia

Southeast Australia

THE GIST: Old-vine Shiraz and Rhône blends

SOIL TYPES: Terra rossa, limestone, sandy clay loam

MAIN VARIETALS: Cabernet Sauvignon, Chardonnay, Grenache, Mourvèdre, Riesling, Shiraz

Victoria

Southeast Australia

THE GIST: Sparkling wines and cool-climate Pinots

SOIL TYPES: Cambrian, granite, red calcareous clay

MAIN VARIETALS: Chardonnay, Muscadelle, Pinot Noir

Western Australia

Southwest Australia

THE GIST: Vibrant Bordeaux-style wines

SOIL TYPES: Gravel, sandy loam

MAIN VARIETALS: Cabernet Sauvignon, Chardonnay, Chenin Blanc, Merlot, Sémillon, Shiraz

SOUTH AFRICA

PAARL
STELLENBOSCH

South Africa has been growing grapes for more than three hundred years, but is now becoming one of the leading New World wine regions. With both warm and cool climates, you can get juicy, high-alcohol reds like Cabernet that rival California's, as well as cooler, highly acidic whites like Sauvignon Blanc. Oh, and South Africa has their own grape! The Pinotage is a cross between Pinot Noir and Cinsault.

Paarl

Southwest South Africa

THE GIST: Rich red wines and tropical white wines

SOIL TYPES: Sandstone, shale, granite

MAIN VARIETALS: Cabernet Sauvignon, Chardonnay, Chenin Blanc, Pinotage, Shiraz

Stellenbosch

Southwest South Africa

THE GIST: Treasure trove of everything from rich wines to easy drinkers

SOIL TYPES: Granite, alluvial sand, sandstone

MAIN VARIETALS: Cabernet Sauvignon, Chardonnay, Chenin Blanc, Merlot, Pinotage, Shiraz

CHILE

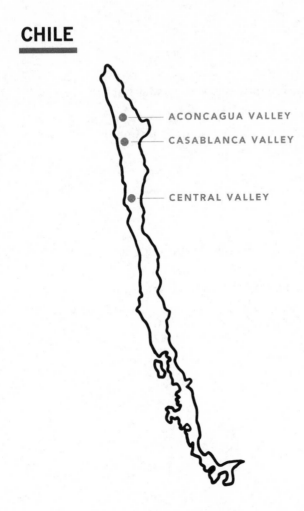

ACONCAGUA VALLEY

CASABLANCA VALLEY

CENTRAL VALLEY

The long and narrow country of Chile is bordered by the Andes Mountains and 2,700 miles of Pacific coastline. And between the two, you have one of the most ideal winegrowing environments, with warm, dry summers and irrigation that occurs naturally from the snow melting off the Andes. Chile is jam-packed full of different terroirs and wine styles, ranging from acid-driven white wines to elegant, age-worthy reds.

Aconcagua Valley

Northern Chile

THE GIST: Hot days and cool nights make for fruit-forward reds

SOIL TYPES: Clay, sand, granite, alluvial

MAIN VARIETALS: Cabernet Sauvignon, Carménère, Merlot, Petit Verdot, Syrah

Casablanca Valley

Northern Chile

THE GIST: Cool-climate, acidic white wines

SOIL TYPES: Sandy loam, clay

MAIN VARIETALS: Chardonnay, Pinot Noir, Sauvignon Blanc

Central Valley

North Central Chile

THE GIST: Large region that has everything from Bordeaux-style reds to experimental whites

SOIL TYPES: Alluvial, granite, clay, loam, gravel

MAIN VARIETALS: Cabernet Sauvignon, Carménère, Merlot, Riesling, Viognier

NEW ZEALAND

New Zealand is one of the most up-and-coming wine regions in New World wines. While they are mostly known for their white wines, all of New Zealand's wines are punctuated with fresh crispness that is indicative of their steadily cool climate.

SOIL TYPES: Greywacke, sandstone, stones, limestone, schist
MAIN VARIETALS: Chardonnay, Pinot Gris, Pinot Noir, Sauvignon Blanc

UNITED STATES

Up until fairly recently, no one thought America could make great wine. Most Americans didn't even think so. As early as 1939, Californian growers started advertising in magazines with illustrations of dolled-up housewives talking about how much their guests loved wine, with slogans like "Be considerate, serve wine!" Despite all the free *How to Cook with Wine* pamphlets the California Wine Advisory Board gave out, no one gave a shit about American wines until 1976. At a wine-tasting competition called the Judgment of Paris,

California wines beat out French wines in blind tastings, propelling American wines to the global stage. Bold Cabernet Sauvignon and oaky Chardonnay became the new gold standard, and eventually American wine's albatross. Today, America is pushing past jam and butter, and even beyond California, with emerging regions in New York and the Pacific Northwest. One might even say we're making America's wine great again.

California

Northern Coast

THE GIST: This region has both classic and oak driven, and light and terroir driven wines.

SOIL TYPES: Clay loam, sandy loam, volcanic, gravel

SUBREGIONS TO GET ACQUAINTED WITH: Mendocino, Napa, Sonoma

MAIN VARIETALS: Cabernet Sauvignon, Chardonnay, Pinot Noir, Sauvignon Blanc

Sierra Foothills

THE GIST: Experimenting with Rhône Valley varietals

SOIL TYPES: Alluvial, loam, rocks, granite

MAIN VARIETALS: Cabernet Sauvignon, Chardonnay, Malbec, Merlot, Petite Sirah, Zinfandel

Central Coast

THE GIST: Most famous for Pinot, but is becoming a hub for Italian styles

SOIL TYPES: Sand, limestone, calcareous, shale, loam, gravel, alluvial

SUBREGIONS TO GET ACQUAINTED WITH: Paso Robles, Santa Barbara, Santa Ynez

MAIN VARIETALS: Cabernet Sauvignon, Chardonnay, Merlot, Pinot Noir, Sangiovese, Syrah

San Diego

THE GIST: No rules, doing as they damn well please

SOIL TYPES: Rock, shale, granitic, sand

MAIN VARIETALS: Carignan, Counoise, Grenache, Petite Sirah, Sangiovese

New York

THE GIST: Badass Rieslings worthy of being aged

SUBREGIONS TO GET ACQUAINTED WITH: Finger Lakes, Long Island

SOIL TYPES: Silt, loam, shale, clay, sand

MAIN VARIETALS: Cabernet Franc, Chardonnay, Concord, French Hybrids (Baco Noir, Seyval Blanc, Vidal Blanc), Gewürztraminer, Merlot, Riesling

Oregon

THE GIST: Cool-climate heaven

SUBREGIONS TO GET ACQUAINTED WITH: Willamette Valley, Southern Oregon

SOIL TYPES: Silt, Jory loam, Willakenzie, gravelly loam

MAIN VARIETALS: Chardonnay, Gamay, Merlot, Pinot Gris, Pinot Noir, Syrah

Washington

THE GIST: Ripe wines full of finesse

SUBREGIONS TO GET ACQUAINTED WITH: Walla Walla, Columbia Valley

SOIL TYPES: Silt, sand, gravel

MAIN VARIETALS: Cabernet Sauvignon, Chardonnay, Merlot, Riesling, Syrah

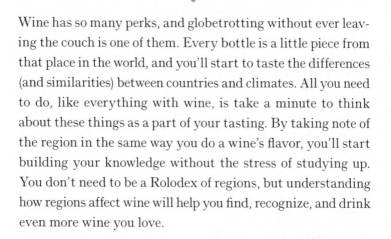

Wine has so many perks, and globetrotting without ever leaving the couch is one of them. Every bottle is a little piece from that place in the world, and you'll start to taste the differences (and similarities) between countries and climates. All you need to do, like everything with wine, is take a minute to think about these things as a part of your tasting. By taking note of the region in the same way you do a wine's flavor, you'll start building your knowledge without the stress of studying up. You don't need to be a Rolodex of regions, but understanding how regions affect wine will help you find, recognize, and drink even more wine you love.

To-Drink List:

1. Think about your favorite wines. Any similarities in the regions? Are they cool climate or warm climate? Old World or New World? Take note of what your favorite wines have in common so you can use those as descriptors for buying or ordering at a restaurant.

2. Try to get a bottle from a region you've never tasted before each time you go shopping for wine. Ask about the terroir and style of the wine, and any other interesting tidbits about what makes this wine from that particular region or vineyard so delicious to whoever is helping you at the wine shop.

3. Practice saying *terroir* for five minutes prior to entering a wine shop and asking about terroir. *Tare-wah tare-wah tare-wah tare-* . . .

CHAPTER SEVEN

Decoding Wine Labels

Reading a wine label is like basically trying to read a foreign language, both figuratively and literally. While I may not be qualified to give you a quick course on the finer points of the Romance languages, I do know my way around a wine label. By law, labels have to give you a certain amount of information about the wine; the good news is you don't even need to understand the language to find it. After this chapter, you will be able to navigate wine labels with ease, rather than the "I'm going to set this shit on fire!" feeling that often accompanies reading an IKEA manual.

There are a few reasons my early wine-imbibing days centered around California wines. Yes, it was because I grew up in California and my parents always drank them. Yes, it was because I was familiar with the regions. Yes, it was because I only got through one week of French class in high school before transferring into Spanish, and the only thing I retained from that class is the ever-crucial *"¿Dónde está la playa?"* But the real reason that I exclusively drank California wines was because I could easily read and understand the labels. I can't tell you how many times I'd look at French wine labels, trying to figure out what kind of wine it was, only to become flustered and grab a California wine with the varietal displayed prominently on the label. Looking back, part of me wishes that I hadn't spent years buying wines based on whether or not the label was written in English. But the bigger part of me knows there's no shame in my wine game, because I'm not alone in this.

Wine labels are intimidating and confusing! You can be looking at a wine label for what feels like hours, a million questions racing through your mind: *Is that the winemaker? Or the region? It sounds like a full name, but considering most of what I know about France I gathered from the opening musical number in* Beauty and the Beast, *I have no fucking idea. Okay, if I can just find out what type of wine this is . . . Why doesn't it just say Chardonnay or whatever? Ugh . . . Where's that cheap Pinot I sort of liked last week?*

I get it. Making sense of a wine label can feel impossible. But those days are behind you. That was before you read this book and got a grasp on varietals, regions, winemaking techniques, and cool shit like how climate affects how a wine tastes. You know what goes into making a bottle of wine; the trick now is learning how to find all that same information on the label. I promise it's all on there.

As with anything, each country has their own way of doing things when it comes to wine labels. Some countries label their wines by winery and varietal, like American wines, and some label their wines by their region, such as French wines. While we will get into specifics about how different labels, well, *label things*, let's start with the basic elements that every wine label has *somewhere* on the label.

The Producer is the winery that grows the grapes and usually makes the wine. On many foreign wines, like French wines, this is usually hidden in tiny text somewhere on the front or back label. On American wines, the producer is found front and center, because we're Americans and that is just how we roll, damn it.

A Name is sometimes used on American wines rather than the producer. This is usually because the wine is produced by a larger winery or corporation and is branded for different audiences. For example, Bronco Wine Company produces more than sixty different wines all under different names, like Charles Shaw, Quail Creek Cellars, or Silver Ridge Vineyards. If it's an American wine, always check the back to see if the producer is listed, although very often the larger producer will not be listed at all.

The Region is where the wine is from. This can be as broad as Bordeaux, or it can be a more specific subregion inside the region of Bordeaux, like Haut-Médoc, or even the exact vineyard where the grapes were harvested. Often, the more specific a wine label is about where the grapes are from, the better the quality of the wine, but this isn't a hard-and-fast rule. I've had many a "Vin de France" I love to death, and that's about as broad as you can get.

The Varietal is the type of grape used, most often listed on the front of New World wines. Some wines can be primarily composed of one varietal blended with a *little* bit of another, but it will list only one varietal on the label. (In other words, a Cabernet blend that is 80 percent Cab and 20 percent

Merlot may just say CABERNET SAUVIGNON on the label.) For Old World wines, the varietal is very rarely listed on the front or back label.

The Appellation is what Old World wines list rather than varietal. An appellation is a government-designated area with specific regulations for what grapes can be grown and what wines can be made. This is why a bottle will say BEAUJOLAIS, but GAMAY is nowhere to be found, because it is known that the region of Beaujolais produces only Gamay by rule of the AOP/AOC. This is confusing for those who buy wine like a Sauv Blanc–seeking missile, but it's totally normal in Europe, where regions are held in high esteem. Always check the back, though, because you may find a varietal hiding in the description.

The Vintage is the year the grapes were harvested. Some wines use grapes harvested from different years; these are considered "nonvintage" wines. Nonvintage (NV) wines are cheaper and are sometimes considered to be of lesser quality, and I tend to agree with that when it comes to buying wine at the grocery store. I've had great nonvintage wines as well, though, so it's always important to talk to your wine shop.

Should You Care about Vintages?

In short: not really. On the one hand, the year grapes were grown and harvested does impact a wine's flavor. Perhaps it was a particularly cold year, so the wines have more acid, or perhaps very hot, so they have higher alcohol percentages. Let's take Olivier Lemasson's "Red Blend" wine as an example. The R13 (for the year it was harvested, 2013) was one of the wines that changed my life, introducing me to how weird wines could get. It smelled like manure and jasmine on damp redwood and tasted like sour, brambly blackberry beer. But the R14 was much softer, tasting more chocolatey and less funky. The year 2013 was a notably shit year for most producers, while 2014 had much better growing conditions. But I loved the one no one loved! So while the year does make a difference, I wouldn't recommend buying or not buying based on "good" or "bad" vintages. If you like a certain producer, they're probably creating great wines you're going to enjoy no matter the year.

Alcohol by Volume (ABV) is the percentage of alcohol in a wine. The higher the alcohol percentage, the riper the grapes were when they were picked, and the richer the wine will be. If you're not a fan of big wines, pay close attention to the ABV. Anything above 14 percent is veering into full-bodied bombs.

Contains Sulfites is something that is only listed on wines in America (both domestic and imported) because in the 1980s, antialcohol lobbyists fought for laws to make alcohol products list their ingredients. The alcohol industry basically said *fuck you,* and we ended up with this warning to placate the lobbyists. All wines have sulfites. ALL OF THEM. I don't care what the white kid with dreadlocks at the farmers' market told you, "sulfite-free" wines are not a thing. Sulfites naturally occur during the fermentation process. Remember, though, that "no added sulfites"—or in French, *"sans soufre"*—wines do exist, and are mostly natural wines.

But Wait! There's More!

On the back! Front labels get most of the love, but make sure to give back labels some attention, too. That is where you will find a wine's importer, and often information you *think* should be on the front label will be hanging out back there. Plus, there's always a chance the winemaker has decided to use that real estate to divulge extra details on the wine or their winemaking practices.

NEW WORLD WINE LABELS

New World labels are very straightforward and are the ones you are probably most familiar with. These labels have the producer/name of the winery and the varietal listed front and center, as well as all of the components I've listed above, but not in any particular manner. Some bottles you'll find the ABV on the front label, some on the back. I've also seen New World wines without front labels at all. It's the wild, wild West but with less Will Smith.

READING NEW WORLD WINE LABELS

PRODUCER

REGION
VINTAGE

GRAPE

ALCOHOL

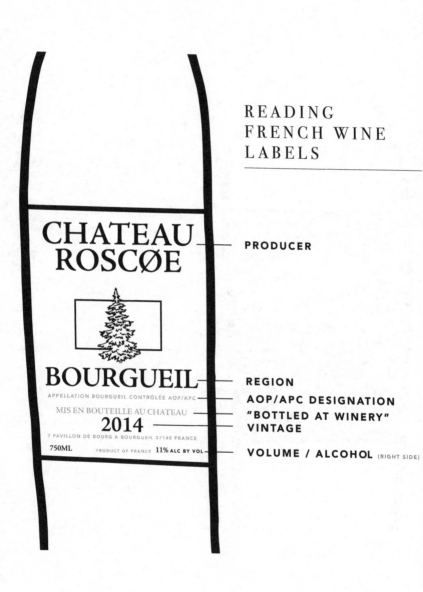

READING
FRENCH WINE
LABELS

PRODUCER

REGION

AOP/APC DESIGNATION

"BOTTLED AT WINERY"

VINTAGE

VOLUME / ALCOHOL (RIGHT SIDE)

FRENCH WINE LABELS

French wine labels draw you in, no doubt about it. You *want* to read them. They're structured, sophisticated, and emanate an air of superiority. This bravado is sexy, but also annoying because French wines assume you *must* know who they are. They're most prominently labeled by region, rarely list the varietal, and to complicate things further, the wines are often blends. France regulates what kind of grapes can be grown in each region, so getting familiar with which regions specialize in which grapes gives you a great advantage when buying them. So yes, when it comes down to it, you must know who they are.

AOP/AOC Classifications

AOP stands for Appellation d'Origine Protégée, which until recently was AOC, Appellation d'Origine Contrôlée. The AOP is a hierarchy of classifications of quality based on a wine's region, their grapes, and how the wine is made. Each region in France sets their own rules as to what is AOP standard. The higher the classification, the stricter the rules, and the better the quality of its wine (in theory). If you're in a grocery store or a shop you're unsure about, you're better off buying a French wine that is AOP classified than a non-AOP wine. The AOP classification system is supposed to take over all European Union wines at some point, although it has yet to happen as of this writing. Here are the classifications you'll see, in order from strictest to no fucks given.

AOP/AOC: This is the highest standard of classification with the strictest rules. A label that says AOP means that the wine comes from a regulated area and meets the region's laws for how the wine must be produced.

IGP (INDICATION GÉOGRAPHIQUE PROTÉGÉE): Classification for larger areas with looser rules, but still playing by the rules.

VIN DE FRANCE OR VIN DE TABLE: NO-RULES WINE. Well, it has to be from France, but it can be from anywhere in France and made any which way. While these can be risky buys in liquor stores, I've had more great Vins de France from my trusted retailers than I can count and many I consider some of my favorite wines.

The Beauj, Though!

Beaujolais has a few of its own designations, and because it's my favorite region, I'm going to tell you about them.

Beaujolais Nouveau: Fresh off the block! This is the first wine made of the year, picked and bottled within a few short months, and traditionally served to celebrate the end of harvest. This is where Beaujolais Nouveau Day comes from each November. While many see Beaujolais Nouveau as a supermarket marketing scheme, *I* see it as an international holiday to honor a timeless grape that runs the gamut from casual to exquisite, as well as a sanctioned day of silence when no one is allowed to give me shit about my Gamay obsession. And it has actual recorded history dating back to WWII, unlike National Waffles Day, which we all know was made up to help people feel better about the unboxed Belgian waffle maker they've been housing in the darkest corner of their cabinet since the holiday gift exchange five years ago.

Beaujolais: This is generic Beaujolais, meaning it's not from a renowned vineyard. That doesn't mean it's not awesome, though. Like anything, it varies from producer to producer.

Beaujolais-Villages: Higher-quality wines made from the thirty-nine authorized villages, recognized for their granite-heavy soils.

Beaujolais Cru: The finest Beaujolais, coming from one of ten specific vineyard sites.

ITALIAN WINE LABELS

It's impossible to say this without coming off like an ironic Urban Outfitters shirt, but it's true: Italians do it better. Their pasta is second to none, their gelato is otherworldly delicious, and I've blown my savings on Italian designer shoes more than once. Whether you're talking sports cars, pizza, flattery, or fashion, Italians are masters. That is, unless we're talking about wine labels. I hate to say it, but Italian wine labels are kind of the worst. They have a few different ways of labeling them, and about a hundred ways just to say "Sangiovese." This wild-card approach makes it as difficult to read their labels as it is to interpret all the talking they do with their hands, but I've got a few tricks for you.

READING ITALIAN WINE LABELS

APPASSIONATO DI SVAGO — PRODUCER

MONTEPULCIANO — GRAPE
—Dᶜ ABRUZZO— — REGION
2015 — VINTAGE

denominazione di origine controlata — CLASSIFICATION
IMBOTTIGLIATO | PIANELLA-ABRUZZO   (L) BOTTLED BY
DA DI SVAGO | ITALIA   (R) PRODUCER / LOCATION
750ML   12.5%ABV   VOLUME / ALCOHOL (RIGHT SIDE)

The diagram showcases a common and traditional label; however, some wines are instead labeled by the grape or by the region. You can usually tell if it's labeled by the grape because the grape will be followed by a *d'* or *di*, followed by the grape's region or subregion, like Barbera d'Asti. A wine labeled by the region will be pretty blatant, like Toscana with its DOC classification (we'll get to that in a sec).

Sangiovese is the most prevalent grape in Italy, but as previously mentioned, there are many, many ways of saying that. All Chianti is Sangiovese, for example. If you see a wine with *Rosso di*, *Vino di*, or something you've never heard of, there's a good chance it's a Sangiovese, too. Make sure to ask your retailer if you're unsure and aren't digging Sangiovese, although I will ask you to reevaluate your life if you're ever in that position. Italian cuisine is a Fellini film, and Sangiovese is a Nino Rota score—straight-up la dolce vita.

DOC Classifications

The Denominazione di Origine Controllata (DOC) is Italy's classification system. Similar to France's AOP system, the DOC was designed to make sure regions follow particular regulations and create quality wines. Each region sets their own rules about what grapes may be grown and how the wines can be made. While Italian wines, like French wines, don't have to follow these rules, a DOC-approved wine is a safer bet. Keep in mind that these classifications may be transitioning to the European Union AOP system over the next couple years.

DOCG (Denominazione di Origine Controllata e Garantita): Classification with the highest standards and strictest regulations to ensure the quality and the authenticity of a wine

DOC (Denominazione di Origine Controllata): Classification for larger areas with looser rules

IGT (Indicazione Geografica Tipica): The loosest set of rules for an Italian wine that is still of good quality, which also allows for non-native grapes like Cabernet Sauvignon or Chardonnay to be used

The important thing to remember is that no matter what country we're talking about, winemakers can make whatever kinds of labels they want. There is no single format for everything. While by law they are required to give you a certain amount of information, they can place it on the bottle however they please, with many winemakers using the labels as an artistic extension of the wines themselves. Once you start getting used to reading the labels, you'll start to be able to pick out these different components no matter how creative a winery gets with it. It feels impossible at times, and believe me, there will always be moments of frustration, but if I've gone from only drinking California Cabernet to being able to decipher Rhône Valley labels, you can, too.

IS BUYING WINE BY THE LABEL REALLY SO BAD?

There you are, walking down the aisle, minding your own business, when it jumps out at you: the most beautiful bottle of wine you've ever laid eyes on. The label is that perfect shade of your favorite color, the one that is a few subtle hues lighter than you can ever find it, the artwork simple but restrained. You pick it up and run your fingers over its debossed lettering, mesmerized. This is the coolest bottle of wine you've ever encountered. How can you *not* buy it?

Your heart is still pumping confetti as you skip to the register, when a dark little cloud of doubt begins to bounce around your brain. You're not supposed to buy wine by the label . . . right? Someone told you that. Didn't they?

The professional wine drinker in me wants to be that someone and say this isn't a good way to buy wine. You should be buying wines based on what information is on the label, like regions and varietals, not because they match a swatch in your Pantone color book. But the consumer in me loves good design work! The truth is, all of us fall victim to buying a bottle because we like the way a label looks. We're only humans! With eyes! And a soft spot for fonts!

If you're in a grocery store or somewhere else with an equally questionable wine selection, please don't buy wines because you like the label. A cool label does not equal a cool wine, and you're going to be paying eight to ten dollars just to be disappointed. Marketers aren't dumb. They know people often buy wines based on the labels, and they design eye-catching labels just for that reason. Often a cool label doesn't mean a new cool producer—it's a new bottling from the same shitty commercial producer you can't stand to drink aside from when you're desperate. When you are shopping for wine at a retailer you are unsure of, always buy based on regions and varietals you like.

But if you're at your wine shop, the wine shop you love and trust, then you can buy wines based on the label all you want. Because that shit is curated! So buy the Italian wine that says nothing but has a cool drawing of a fish! Buy the French wine you can't read not only because you don't know French, but it is also written in a wildly illegible, scribbly font! Buy whatever the hell you think looks cool, because there is a much better chance it's actually cool when you're getting it from a retailer that you know isn't serving you second-label swill.

Or say fuck that and go right ahead and buy the bottle.

After all, it *is* your favorite color.

Neither of us learned Italian in the span of this chapter, but that's all right, because you learned you don't need to in order to buy a good bottle of wine. Getting comfortable with wine labels is so important for informed wine buying, because all the information is right there for you. The more you look for the info, the easier it becomes to see it. So much more reliable than crossing your fingers in hopes this is one of those white wines you like.

These were only a handful of the labels you'll see in your

wine drinking, but with this foundation, you'll be able to handle labels from countries near and far, some that are very cool and some that are more poorly designed than an Angelfire website from 1999.

But remember: Never judge a wine by its subpar design. I've had some killer biodynamic wines that had labels that looked like they were originally designed for dentists' outdoor signs in suburban office parks. Wine bottles, like people, should always be judged by what's on the inside, not by the terrible decision to use Comic Sans.

To-Drink List:

1. Take whatever wine you currently have in your house and dissect the label. Locate the producer/name, region, varietal, vintage, and importer (or all that are applicable).

2. Next time you're shopping for wine, apply this practice by inspecting wines you're browsing. If you start to feel overwhelmed, take a deep breath and remember that everything you need to know is on the label (and you know it all).

3. Buy the one with the cool label. You know you want to. Unless you're at Target. You're already buying aesthetically irresistible shit you weren't planning on buying. Stick to the throw blanket that mysteriously ended up in your cart, and hit up the wine store on your way home instead.

CHAPTER EIGHT

Buying & Ordering Wine

If there's one feeling that all wine drinkers experience, it is the anxiety that accompanies buying it. You know what I'm talking about. You're on a last-minute mission to grab a bottle before a dinner party. But should you bring red? White? Wait, did they say their mom was coming? Doesn't their mom love . . . Shit! What is that wine their mom loves?! You scan the aisle for a familiar label to save you, but you are alone and overwhelmed by all the options. The shelves start to close in, and paranoia begins to creep up. Suddenly, you feel very stoned even though you didn't smoke anything. "The clerk, he's watching, isn't he? He knows I know nothing about wine, doesn't he? DOESN'T HE?!" You pick up a bottle and pretend to read it, like you somehow learned French in the last two minutes. The only thing you can decipher on the label is the price tag, which is even scarier than asking for help. You grab the most appealing and legible label within arm's reach and get the hell out of there, never to return. Except you're back two days later buying more wine, complicit in your own reoccurring nightmare.

Same thing with restaurants, too. There you are, settling

into a table with your friends, the carefree Friday night feeling swelling up inside you. You're finally at ease after a hell of a week, when the host decides to strike you with the fear of God by handing you a wine list the size of a Bible. You try to pass it on to one of your friends, but they wave you off, joyfully recalling that one time (the only time) you ordered a good bottle (accidentally). You start to flip through the list, looking for something cheap but not too cheap because hey, you're not cheap! But you're also not rich. The sommelier sees you flailing and comes by to literally look down on you. You pull together what little poise you have in you and point to the second-cheapest bottle, fingers crossed that everyone likes it. Spoiler alert: They don't. You don't! And then everyone switches to cocktails, and you are never left with the wine list again.

These situations are enough to scare some people into sticking with vodka sodas for the rest of their lives. But not you. You know that what doesn't shame us into never drinking wine again only makes us stronger. Also neither of these scenarios could ever be as embarrassing as when that popular girl tricked you into grabbing a soda can off the top of the garbage and then got everyone to chant, "TRASH DIGGER! TRASH DIGGER!" even though you didn't fucking dig through the trash! The can was on top! And you lived through that (and the rest of eighth grade), so you've got this.

After this chapter, you will rise to these occasions like a pro wine-drinking Phoenix. You will frequent wine shops you used to be afraid of, more often than spin class. You will be throwing your hand up faster than Hermione Granger with a right answer to volunteer for bringing the wine. You'll take the wine list at restaurants with a Zen-like quality usually reserved for monks, or people with Xanax prescriptions. And you will feel fucking great.

When I started buying wine, like most people, I dreaded coming off like a dumbass. But I knew that was inevitable, considering I didn't know anything about wine except that I liked it red and cheap. So rather than fight it, I decided to own it. I embraced my ignorance with enthusiasm, wearing it like a badge of honor that was also a neon crossing-guard vest. No one could miss it, because every conversation in a wine shop started with me telling someone I knew nothing about wine. And while this tactic started as a way to protect myself from feeling judged or shamed, I began to feel a power in it. Because I had nothing to prove, I wasn't afraid to ask a million questions. *What's a Jura? Why would anyone oxidize wines on purpose? Do you have anything that tastes like cranberry juice and Pop Rocks? What's supercheap but doesn't supersuck?*

With every explanation of a different fermentation and every bottle I drank of a grape I'd never heard of, I was gaining an education. Each piece of information I picked up made me feel stronger, more excited, and more inquisitive in ways I may never have if I had approached wine with an ego. By admitting I knew nothing, I gave myself the freedom to learn.

And I want you to feel the same way, too.

Far too often as adults, we're expected to know it all, or at least pretend we do. Sometimes you need to—like at a new job when your boss asks you to put together a PowerPoint and you say, "Absolutely!" even though you haven't touched the program since you were presenting arguments to your parents about how a Tamagotchi was essential to "understanding responsibility." But for enjoyable things your paycheck doesn't depend on, like wine, the only thing your pretending to know it all will do is keep you from learning anything. Instead of hiding your inexperience, be emboldened by your curiosity. Rather than focus on how much you don't know, get excited about all there is to discover. Take pride in your new passion and own that shit.

THE IMPORTANCE OF A WINE SHOP

If there's one thing that I want you to take away from this book, it is that it is *imperative* for you to find a good wine shop. Not a bodega, not the chain store with 20 percent off six or more bottles—I'm talking about a shop that is strictly dedicated to selling wine (and perhaps some beer and spirits, too). It may not be the first store you walk into, but once you find your wine shop, it's like finding your Cheers, but better, because you get to take the wine home with you.

Wine shops may seem intimidating, but they are generally filled with nice people who love wine and love talking about wine. It pours out of them joyfully and effortlessly; a single question can spiral into bite-size history lessons, tales of tastings, and recollections of cars breaking down outside the Loire Valley during French gas strikes. Shop employees can take a vague, thirty-second conversation with you about how you're looking for a red to pair with your dinner, and turn it into six rousing recommendations you can't bear to choose amongst. Not because they're trying to upsell you, but because they genuinely are so excited about wine that they can't contain themselves. When you combine their enthusiasm and experience with their knowledge of what's on their shelves, the people who work in wine shops are the most reliable to buy wine from. All it takes is talking to them.

Which is the scary part for many, I know. I promise I'm not trying to be your overly outgoing wingman friend at the bar, pressuring you to "Just go talk to them!" before pushing you out onto the dance floor, leaving you all blush-faced and alone. But it's something you really need to start doing. Unlike us consumers who have a great wine and then get too drunk to really remember what it tasted like besides "supergood," the people in wine shops know tasting notes like your brother knows sports stats. They are constantly talking about them, and so you should be constantly talking to *them*. Communication is key.

Breaking the Ice at a Wine Shop

Sometimes it's not that simple to "just go talk" to people. I have terrible social anxiety, but oddly enough, it makes me *more* talkative. While that makes it easier for me to chat up strangers about Syrah, I understand how scary it feels and how hard it can be. The more you talk to people in wine shops, the easier it gets, I promise. But you have to get started somewhere, so here's some easy ways to break the ice, and a few tips to help you stay cool and calm in your convo.

➤ "How's it going?" rolls off the tongue more naturally than rushing to ask where the Gewürztraminer is. It starts a friendly, low-pressure dialogue so you can warm up a little before they ask you what you're looking for.

➤ "Hi, I'm looking for . . ." is good if small talk makes you want to barf. Straight to the point and, hopefully, straight to a delicious bottle!

➤ "Can you point me in the direction of . . ." helps open a conversation you can come back to, but it also gives you an out to go look at labels alone.

➤ "I'm reading this book and it says I have to talk to you . . ." I haven't personally used this one, but feel free to blame me!

➤ If you don't know how to pronounce something, just say so! By acknowledging it, you're owning it, and you're much less likely to be embarrassed.

➤ If you mispronounce something, just laugh. It will suck the stress out of the situation, and the shopkeeper will most assuredly relate and giggle along with you.

➤ Know that anything you're embarrassed about, no one else gave it a second thought. Everyone is the center of their own universe, so while you may be replaying that awkward moment in the white-wine aisle over and over in your head, the other person is most likely fixated on how to recover from all the drunk texts they sent their crush last night.

Finding the right wine shop for you is a lot like finding "your record store." Maybe the first record you grab is a dud, or maybe there's a metal section you would never buy anything from, but that doesn't mean they don't have that Elvis record you've been looking for or that weird bossa nova album you took a chance on that is now the only thing you spin. But you would never know if you just went in the one time and said, "EW, METAL!" and walked out. Nor does getting an original pressing of *Pet Sounds* at a record store automatically mean it's the best fucking record store of all fucking time.

With wine shops, you need to give it a couple visits and try multiple bottles. You want to be able to get an idea of their overall style, from the wines they stock to their customer service. And when you find one with an overall style you dig, it is THE BEST. It's like shopping online knowing everything is going to fit. Or how every episode—*any episode!*—of that one show will make you laugh. Or like if you came every time you had sex, or at least got *pretty damn close* and still enjoyed it immensely. That's how good finding a wine shop you love is. No matter what you choose, you're going to be satisfied. Or at least "get it" and feel good about it, because you know their style, and you trust it.

I trust my favorite wine shops so much you would assume I was of blood relation to their owners. Places like Domaine LA, Lou, or Ordinaire know me better than I know myself. I will try anything they recommend, and I will walk around picking appealing labels off the shelves without even looking at what type of wine it is. I wouldn't do that anywhere else, because the outcome of such impetuous shopping would be as gratifying as me lighting a ten-dollar bill on fire. But at my favorite wine shops, I know what they like to buy. And goddamn, do I like to drink it. Even when the wine isn't something I would drink regularly, I still appreciate it.

I want that relationship for you. I want you to have the coolest older brother of a wine store that will impart knowledge and introduce you to dope shit you never knew existed. Unfortunately, we're not all born with cool older brothers, and none of us are born with cool older brother wine shops. You have to go out there and not only find them but be an active customer. It's a legit relationship: It takes time, it takes effort, it takes openness, and it takes trust. But I promise you will drink what you sow.

HOW I BUY WINE & YOU SHOULD, TOO

As much as I wish I sat upon a golden throne of wine while producers cast bottles at my feet to drink at my leisure, that is not the case. Literally not the case, because I, like others, go to a wine shop and buy that case myself with my hardearned dollars.* Unlike other tasks, though, this is not an errand for me. It is a goddamned delight.

---

* Full Disclosure: I do get offered free wine, but I rarely take it. For one, the wine that people want to send me is not usually the type of wine I like to drink. I'm not going to waste their product, or increase my carbon footprint, by having it sent to me when I know damn well I'm going to go buy some wild-ass Pineau d'Aunis that I will love to death. Second, I don't like feeling indebted to anyone. If I like the wine, I like it. I don't write about things I don't like, and I don't like people making me feel that I should. Also because sometimes I'm just busy, and then I feel like an asshole for drinking the wine and not writing about it. I don't have time to feel like an asshole . . . but we'll save that for my self-help book (Plume, 2030).

I skip into my shops like a character from a musical, eyes sparkling with hope and a belly full of butterflies. Perhaps I'll meet a rugged Italian I've never heard of, or an electric-coral-colored bubbly I can't take my eyes off of! And there's always the chance the new Jean Foillard Morgon "Côte du Py" vintage is in, sitting there like an old lover I never thought I'd see again, looking better than ever. To me, shopping for wine elicits a mixture of the innocent eagerness and surprise of the first day of school, and the thrill of being on the prowl to take something home for the night.

My strategy varies depending on what occasion I'm buying the wine for, but when it comes to my personal, on the reg, wine-buying habits, I have one rule that I must follow. It's the easiest rule in this entire book, so you have no excuse not to follow it, too: I walk into my wine shop and ask a series of questions.

"What's new? What's good?" I treat buying wine like I treat buying produce at a farmers' market: I want what is fresh and seasonal. Wines that are new to the shop are often the freshest on the staff's mind. They most likely have recently tasted it and are excited about it, so they can tell you a lot about it. Recent arrivals are also very often seasonal, like rosé in the spring and Beaujolais Nouveau in the fall. Not only do they pair well with the weather, but they are likely to pair well with what's actually in season at the farmers' market and what ends up on your plate. But most important, buying something that is new to the store and new to you means you are constantly learning.

"What are you drinking?" Since the wine shop employees are tasting wine all day, the wines they want to go home and drink are usually pretty special. Not "special" as in pricey or rare, special in that they are simply delicious. Trying other people's favorite wines not only expands your palate, but it also helps you understand their tastes. One dude may be super into orange wines, while another lady may always be drinking gritty Spanish wines. This is all useful knowledge to tuck away and use when you need to ask someone about specific recommendations in the future.

"What's like . . ." We all have our favorite wine, but you're not going to learn much if you drink the same thing all the time. Always ask for something that's *like* what you love but from a different producer or region. This shows you the many variations a wine can have, and helps you identify characteristics as they vary by region, fermentation, and terroir. Plus, a dozen favorite Gamays is better than one favorite Gamay.

"What's weird?" This may not be for everyone, but I want the wackiest shit in the joint. Whatever bottle is the most out-there, haven't-heard-of-this, never-knew-this-was-possible—that's a bottle for me. Curiosity may have killed the cat, but it just gets me drunk and excited to research what makes the wine so different. *Weird* may not be the adjective for you, but find the types of wine that intrigue you and explore them as often as possible.

After asking these questions, I take all the recommendations into consideration, and pick out the one(s) I would like to try. I know the questions seem simple and small-talkish, but they are effective because they keep you trying new things and could lead you to stumble upon your new favorite wine. One of my more recent favorite wines is a wine called Wah-wah, by Brendan Tracey. It's a Loire Valley red blend that I became obsessed with, quite possibly even addicted to. Thinking about it right now is making my mouth water and my loins tingle. It was everything I ever wanted in a wine—tart, gluggy, slightly carbonite, youthful. I drank it more regularly than water because it was a constant reminder as to why I started to write about wine to begin with: It's delicious and it makes me happy. But I never would have found it had I not walked into Lou with my questions. Remember that the best bottles of wine may be as easy to find as it is easy for you to ask, "What's new? What's good?"

DOLLARS & SENSE

If you're thinking, *"Well, Marissa, cool advice but guess what. I'm not walking into a wine shop and spending a bajillion dollars on new, 'weird' wines."* Don't worry, I'm not either.

When buying wine, it's important to be up front about your budget. I know, I know, it feels icky. No one likes talking about money, but you *gotta* do it. I can't tell you how many times I've walked into a wine shop and announced I have approximately $50 to my name. Embarrassing? A little, but only because I'm an idiot with money, not because I'm not in the market for a $200 bottle of Burgundy. Most people buying wine are on a budget, and not only is it not weird to make your budget a part of your wine-buying criteria, it's absolutely necessary.

Let's say you walk into a wine shop, asking what's new, what's good, what this particular shop employee likes to drink.

If they are suggesting wines that are out of your price range, you need to tell them so you're not wasting their time or yours. After all, there's nothing worse than going through the whole process of having someone show you a bunch of stuff you're never going to buy, and then having to grab something cheap in a hurry that you know nothing about. When you're asking your questions, or giving specifics on what you're looking for, throw in a quick "I'm looking in the fifteen-dollar price range" or "Something under thirty dollars" or "SKY'S THE LIMIT, PAL, MAMA GOT PAID! But no, seriously, let's keep it around fifty dollars." There are wonderful wines being made at all price points, and by being honest about what you can spend, you will get recommendations that are not only delicious but affordable.

Don't Believe the Hype

You know those WINNER OF BEST PINOT GRIGIO! stickers? Ignore them. Those competitions are judged by a roomful of wine industry people who are speed-tasting dozens of commercial wines that paid to be in the competition. So it's not the "best" out of all the wines in the world, simply of the wineries rich enough to participate. And while we're at it, those 100-point ratings? Don't put any stock in that shit either. It's all subjective, and just because some random old dude gave a wine a low rating doesn't mean you wouldn't give it 110. A great example of this is California winemaker Michael Cruse's cult sparkling wine, Ultramarine. It got an 84-point rating, but it is the most coveted American sparkling wine and Cruse was named Winemaker of the Year by the *San Francisco Chronicle* in 2016. The only awards and ratings to trust are your own.

BUYING LOW-INTERVENTION WINES

How do you know who to trust? Always start by looking at the label. While they aren't showy about it, many low-intervention wines give you clues. On the front, it may say SANS SOUFRE or NO ADDED SULFITES. On the back, it may mention handpicked grapes, a no-pesticides policy, or allude to minimal interference. But the most important thing to look at is the importer and/or distributor. It's not something most people think about, but on the back of a wine, there is always some sort of indication of who imported and/or distributed the wine. Sometimes it's on the label itself, often buried amongst other small print, or sometimes it's a separate sticker, but if you're buying wine, it's definitely there.

Some of the most unsung heroes in the wine game, importers and distributors are the people who get the wines you drink into the stores. An importer is licensed to bring wine into the country from foreign countries, and a distributor is someone who is licensed to sell the wines within the country. While distributors may work with many importers, an importer themselves may also be a distributor. Having a wine store you trust and love is the best way to shop for wines, but being familiar with importers/distributors is a close second. Importers and distributors have portfolios of wines they represent, and they usually have a certain style they specialize in. When it comes to those who represent low-intervention wines, even if not every single wine in their book is certified organic or biodynamic or whatever, you can guarantee that they are very close in quality.

While it's impossible to know every winemaker, it is possible to know a handful of importers and distributors you like. When you start paying attention, you'll notice a pattern that the wines you like are probably all imported and distributed by the same people over and over again. This is such a fantastic way to shop for wine, because even if you're in a store you've never visited before, you can look for importers and distributors you trust. And this isn't just for natural wines, but in general. Shopping for wines by importers and/or distributors you are familiar with gives you a great idea of what kind of wine you're buying.

For example: In Kermit Lynch We Trust. Never forget that. I trust Kermit Lynch more than most people I know. The legendary importer, distributor, and author (who you should definitely read in your ongoing pursuit of wine knowledge) started selling unadulterated and terroir-driven wines in the early 1970s. He's also the guy that started using refrigerated shipping containers so wines being imported wouldn't be spoiled by heat. While he is not married to natural wines, he is dedicated to wines of pure character that are reflective of where they were grown and who they are grown by. It wouldn't be a stretch to say that we would not have many of the European-style easy-drinking wines that I love so dearly if Lynch had not persevered throughout the Parker years of heavy oak and monster Cabs. I know that anything he puts his name on is of quality, from $12 fizzy Italian blends to pricey French magnums.

Importers/Distributors to Be on the Lookout for in Your Search for Low-Intervention Wines:

Amy Atwood Selections
Goatboy Selections
Jenny & François Selections
Kermit Lynch
Louis/Dressner Selections
Nomadic Distribution
Percy Selections
Rosenthal
Savio Soares Selections
Selection Massale
SelectioNaturel
Sylvester/Rovine

BUYING WINE FOR YOURSELF

There are plenty of reasons why you could be buying wine for yourself. Perhaps you finished a big project, bought a new throw blanket you want to snuggle up with, or maybe it's because *sommmeone* drank it all (it was your dick roommate). Whatever the reason may be, you need to hit the wine shop. While wandering around asking questions is a great way to get cool new stuff, sometimes you want a little guidance dictated by mood. Here are some suggestions to treat yourself.

For a Long Day/Week/Month/Life

It's been a long one. You are weary, emotional, and very likely in need of some sweatpants. First, my condolences. Second, you want a spicy red wine that leaves you feeling all sorts of warm and fuzzy, like a **Syrah** or a **Zinfandel**. These wines feel like custom-fitted onesies for your soul while you rewatch your favorite season of *Seinfeld* and remember that everything is going to be all right.

For Small Successes & Big Wins

Sparkling wine, of course. Not only does it physically embody the idea of bursting with excitement, it pairs exceptionally well with a sense of accomplishment and turning Kanye all the way up. If you're celebrating finishing a mind-numbing project like doing your taxes or reorganizing your closet, get **Cava**. Made just like Champagne but at half the cost, you get all the fun without the price tag. If you're celebrating life-changing events like job promotions, graduations, or anything love or baby related, get **Champagne**. Don't even play like you weren't already planning to. It's rare when you have a legitimate reason to splurge, so take it. Either way, pop that shit and cheers to you. You deserve it.

For Pre-Gaming a Big Night Out

Before you hit the town, you want something that is energetic enough to incite some serious post-shower-underwear-mirror dancing, but also mellow enough to have a glass on the couch before hopping in the taxi. Always choose something chilled because the last thing you need after getting ready is to get all hot with a heavy red. I always go **Vinho Verde**, easy drinking but fizzy enough to give a regular Friday a festive vibe.

For After a Date

"Would you like to come in?" should always be followed with something as intriguing as those implications. Something smooth but dirty, and as alluring as it is energetic. **Carignan** is deliciously dusty and juicy all at once, and is just as sexy to have all to yourself as it is to share.

For Being Fucking Sad

While wine makes us super happy, it's technically a downer and rarely helps with being sad. Self-medicating is not chill, but we've all been in a place where we just want our pj's, a large pie delivered to our doorstep, a good cry, and a better wine. In these situations, I like to lean on the shoulders of medium-bodied wines like **Barbera**. This wine is an agreeable companion that loves pizza just as much as you do and will listen to you instead of trying to convince you to cheer up (ugh, if only more people were as understanding as wine; JUST LET ME FEEL HOW I FEEL).

For a Night In

Tonight? You can't. You're just soooo busy. You have dates back to back with every face mask you own. And it's not like your favorite TV shows are going to watch themselves. Plus, you haven't filled up shopping carts of shit you can't afford online lately, and someone has to smoke this joint before it goes bad. The only things you have time for are picking up some **Pineau d'Aunis** and hopping in the bath.

Just for Drinking

The wine you keep around your house for casual drinking should be like that one friend that is always down for whatever. It's down for drinking on a warm afternoon, down for drinking with dinner, down for drinking in bed. **Gamay** is the natural choice. You can throw it in the fridge, you can pair it with anything, and you won't go bankrupt keeping it stocked.

BUYING WINE FOR FAMILY

Buying wine for family is just like doing anything with family. It's all about navigating the path of least resistance, and avoiding politics. The goal is to keep everyone happy and everything on the light side. Perhaps you have a great relationship with your family, and you can totally be yourself and not make any waves, in which case, great! Take that unfiltered **Chardonnay** to your radically conservative uncle's birthday! Me? I love my family, and we're all on good terms (outside of election years), but I don't want to get into it with them trying to explain the merits of a biodynamic orange wine that smells like piss and tastes like a sour Red Bull. It would inevitably devolve into how I'm an artsy liberal and before you know it, I'm calling people racist and am being disowned. Again. I don't have time to deal with getting un-disowned, so here are my safe bets that my family will love and I can enjoy with them without potentially setting a trash can on fire at the dinner table.

For Steak-Loving Dads

If your father fancies himself a grill master, he loves **Cabernet**. This is a fact, because if he is your dad then he lived through the nineties, and you could not live through the nineties and love steak and not love Cabernet. Actual fact: Cabernet pairs really well with steak, so even if he's not in love with it, he will still appreciate it. If your dad also watches (sleeps through) golf on Saturday afternoons, get a bottle that Robert Parker has reviewed. Robert Parker's reviews mean nothing to us but they mean a lot to dads who love golf. If your dad doesn't love golf, then get a new California Cabernet. They're a bit lighter than the steakhouse Cabs of the Bill Clinton era. If your dad is cool and into trying new things, get **Mourvèdre**.

For "Wine"-Loving Moms

You know who I'm talking about. They are the moms that have all sorts of wine paraphernalia, like signs that say LIVE • LAUGH • WINE or magnets that have fifties housewives on them with jokes about how just like wine, they get better with age. Always go with a light and fruity white wine that can be drank in the afternoon, and can take a few ice cubes if Mom feels so inclined. **Pinot Grigio** and **Chenin Blanc** are slam-dunk mom wines, but bring a **Viognier** if you want to surprise her.

For Hippie Sisters

Every family has that one de facto stoner who may or may not be going to Burning Man for the sixth year in a row. They are my favorite people to buy wine for because they are totally down with weird stuff. Bring a bottle of orange wine to share while they explain the new yoga they're teaching and why you have to wash your crystals a certain way. They will be delighted by how much it tastes like their roommate's homemade kombucha.

For Total Bro[thers]

I once was in an airport bar next to a bro. He was drinking a beer at 7:00 A.M., me a mimosa. We started chatting and he looked around, as if to tell me a secret, before saying, "Don't tell anyone, but I really love to cook for myself and open a nice **Malbec**." Sorry, guy, I'm now telling everyone, because *lots* of bros love a nice Malbec. They're full-bodied, bold, and go well with things like brisket. They are also recognizable and trendy, so as to not disturb the fragility of the bro ego.

For Super-Religious Aunts

Avoid anything red. No need to incite a lecture on abortion because you're sipping on the blood of Christ. She probably doesn't drink much, so choose a sweeter white like **Moscato** that is easy for non–wine lovers to enjoy and also tastes a bit like dessert. A wonderful way to talk about all the baking you've been doing, and not talk about how you're officiating a gay wedding next weekend.

For Cousins You Don't Really Know, but Are Cool With

You don't know their favorite movies or their dogs' names, but you do share blood and plenty of childhood memories. **Sangiovese** is easy to throw back and tastes like the holidays, making it perfect for reminiscing, gossiping, and smoking weed in the back of your car in your grandmother's driveway like a dumb teenager. It's all about bonding, and then not seeing each other again until the next holiday when you get wine drunk and say you guys *really* should see each other more often.

For the Political One

Whichever side of the political spectrum you're on, there is bound to be someone in your family who is the exact opposite of you. And while you love them, you often must suppress the urge to murder them once you start sharing your thoughts on the world. Bring **Pinot Noir**. With its moderate tannins, acidity, and use of oak, Pinot is a bipartisan champion that most people can agree to agree on.

BUYING WINE FOR FRIENDS, AND PEOPLE YOU DON'T REALLY KNOW BUT YOU'RE GOING TO THEIR PARTY AND DON'T WANT TO LOOK LIKE A DICK

Buying wine for friends, or even friends of friends, is the most fun a person can have aside from buying wine for themselves. Mostly because you will probably still get to drink it. Get ready for a good time, because regardless of whether or not you have anything to wear, you've got good wine.

For Your Best Friend Who Refuses to Drink Anything but Pinot

Can't fault anyone for knowing what they like, except you can in this situation, because only drinking one type of wine is ridiculous. This is your best friend! You can't let them live this way! They're denying themselves happiness! Sort of like the people they choose to date! And while you can't trick them into better relationships, you *can* trick them into trying new wines. I don't normally encourage trickery, but your pal would benefit greatly from you slyly pouring them a red blend from **Cheverny**. The French region's rouge wines blend Pinot Noir, Gamay, Cabernet Franc, Côt, and Pineau d'Aunis. It's similar enough so that they won't immediately reject it, and just different enough for you to make the case for expanding their horizons.

For a Hang Sesh with a New Friend

You have mutual friends, you like the same bands, you both like *Bob's Burgers*. Or at least one of those things. You don't really know this person, but you know enough to have drunkenly made plans that you are intending to keep. Bring your favorite reasonably priced wine to see how much you *really* have in common.

For a Small Dinner Party with Close Friends

Always ask the host what they need or want. If they say "Whatever!" ask what they are cooking and make an informed decision (see pairing chapter). If they haven't decided on the menu, bring **Lambrusco**. Guaranteed your other friends will bring red, white, or rosé, and Lambrusco will add an unexpected splash of spontaneity to the evening. Everyone loves bubbles, especially when there's nothing to celebrate except one another's company.

For a Big Dinner Party with Mostly Randos

You know the host, but you don't know 75 percent of the other attendees, and the host isn't answering any of your texts, so you have no idea what they're cooking. This could be stressful, except you know you're bringing **Dry Riesling**. Riesling is hands-down the most food-friendly wine in the game, and is a lifesaver in situations you're unsure about. Nearly everyone likes Riesling, but inevitably, one of these random humans you're having a meal with will say, "Oh, no Riesling for me. It's too sweet." You will then have the joy of explaining that many Rieslings are dry, pouring them a small taste, and watching their whole life change right before your eyes.

For a Birthday Party of a Friend of a Friend

Rosé. Everyone loves rosé.

For a Shitty House Party You Got Dragged To

Yo, you don't know any of these people. Do not roll in with your favorite wine, thinking you're going to be able to share and enjoy it with people who give a shit. It is more likely that you will get one glass before some dude with a Tecate carts it off to the backyard for his girlfriend, never to be seen again. Bring **Grüner Veltliner**. It's affordable and often comes in liters, increasing the chance that you will actually get to drink it.

BUYING WINE TO SHARE WITH YOUR SIGNIFICANT OTHER

Buy their favorite wine and drink it gladly. Buy your favorite wine and show them why you love it. Buy a wine you both have never tried and put on your favorite record and look lovingly into each other's eyes. Just drink wine and have awesome sex. The End.

BUYING WINE FOR A GIFT

Gifting wine is different than bringing wine over. Bringing wine over is a cool way of saying, "Thanks for having me, I want to contribute/mostly want to drink this with you." Gifting wine is saying, "Yo, this is an actual present just for you and whatever you want to do with it, although if you want to open it with me you can, but you definitely do not have to because it's a present. For you."

The natural tendency in this situation is to buy something you know for sure that they like. But buying what someone always drinks is boring, and leaves the gift feeling hollow. Instead, aim to buy a wine that incorporates that person's tastes as well as something you love about wine. That way, you're pretty damn sure they're going to enjoy it, but it also gives them a new wine experience. If you buy what you know they like, there isn't much they can say besides they liked it. By purchasing something that's a little different, and includes something you are passionate about with wine, it opens up a conversation. Maybe you bought it because you love the producer or the region, or maybe because it reminds you of that time the two of you went to see the Strokes. Whatever the reason, it's sharing a little piece of yourself with that person.

And you *must* wrap this wine so it won't be confused with regular old "bringing over" wine. You put care into this bottle, and you want it to be truly enjoyed by its recipient. You don't want Hayley from your homie's HR department who you just met five minutes ago popping and pouring it like it's some corner-store shit you grabbed in a hurry. Wrapping is essentially a fancy sticky note reading, "I WILL RAIN HELL ON YOUR RUDE ASS IF YOU DARE OPEN THIS." So invest in some ribbon, and start saving all the brown paper bags the wine shop sends you home with. I have a whole *drawer* dedicated to saved brown paper wine bags and ribbon. It is the most adult thing about me. I can barely file expense reports, but I am prepared at any moment to transform a bottle of wine into a thoughtful gift.

There's purpose to doing this beyond aesthetics, too. Wrapping it signals to the host that they don't have to serve it. Maybe they don't want to serve it because they know Hayley is going to drink it all, or maybe they don't want to serve it because they already have their wines planned out for the evening. Whatever the reason, the recipient should feel they can enjoy it when they want to enjoy it. If that is immediately upon receiving it, great! Unless you already know about Hayley and her absentminded boozehounding, in which case a quick whisper of "Hey, you should save this for when you can really enjoy it!" is never frowned upon.

HOW TO ORDER WINE IN ANY RESTAURANT

You open the wine list, and your heart jumps. And then it thuds. Did it just hit your stomach? Or did that knot show up all on its own? With sweaty palms, you flip through the leather-bound book full of names that sound more like private schools plucked from Wes Anderson films than actual wineries. "Seeing anything you like?" the sommelier asks, knowing damn well you couldn't tell a Sancerre from your own asshole. Now you've got this guy reading over your shoulder and breathing suggestions down your neck, and while he may be earnestly trying to help you, it's only making your palms sweatier and that knot tighter and all you want to do is close your eyes, put your finger on a random bottle, and pray it's in your price range.

I don't blame you. Wine lists are the worst. They're all organized differently, or not organized at all, just catalogs of words you've never seen before, separated by commas. Even when you know quite a bit about wine, most lists you encounter are still going to have tons of shit you've never heard of. And often, it's *only* shit you've never heard of. To this day, it's not unlikely for me to open a wine list and have less leads than a bad hand of Clue.

It's important to ditch the notion that ordering wine at a restaurant is about ordering a bottle you know. Instead, ordering wine at a restaurant is about strategically finding a bottle that is best for you and your food. Here are all the tactics you need to conquer wine lists with confidence.

1. **Get an idea of what you're going to eat first.** I know, I know, I know. You just got off work and you can't wait to get a glass in front of you, chill out, and forget about that stupid meeting, but don't rush to order. Wine is meant to complement food, so don't jump to the wine list without opening the menu first. You don't want to order some gnarly bold red and then realize the ceviche is calling your name. If you simply cannot wait, start with a glass of something light and acidic that will get your taste buds revved up but won't exhaust your palate before you even order your entrée.

2. **Be careful not to overwhelm your palate.** Speaking of palates . . . It feels like second nature to order a bombastic red for dinner, but wines with heavy tannins, oak, or alcohol obliterate your taste buds. Be cautious when ordering big bold wines like Cabernet, Petite Sirah, or Malbec if you want to actually taste your dinner along with your vino.

3. **Look to see if they specialize in a certain type or region of wine.** When you open the wine list, is it 96 percent California wines? If so, you should probably order a California wine. The restaurant may have a handful of French wines, but it's only to please that one stuck-up couple a night that refuses to drink anything but *le best*. Same thing if you notice mostly Rieslings, for example. A restaurant carries wines that they feel go best with their food, so take their lead.

4. **Look for varietals and regions you know and love.**

While you may not recognize any producers on the list, there's a good chance you will know some grapes and places. Finding a few familiar faces gives you something to fall back on if you don't find anything else you want, but they're also a great reference for when you . . .

5. **Talk to the waiter/sommelier.** You have to! This ain't Vegas! And even if it was, you wouldn't roll up to the craps table and throw $80 on "Horn high 12!" when you don't even know what that means! You **must** talk to the waiter/sommelier, even if it intimidates you. Just tell them what you like and what you don't, point out those varietals and regions you love, and tell them your price range. You don't have to take their suggestions, but having their recommendations and some insight is a much smarter bet than putting your money down blindly.

6. **Don't worry about looking cheap.** Unless you're into some advanced-level Buddhist shit, there's often a tinge of embarrassment when mentioning a budget. Forget this. Life's not all scallops and Champagne— there are bills to be paid and cat litter to be bought! Asking a waiter/sommelier about what works in your price range is nothing to be ashamed of. It helps ensure you're going to get something great that won't break the bank, rather than hurriedly ordering one that's cheap but not, like, *too cheap*.

If you really don't want the rest of your party knowing how much you're willing to spend on a bottle, you can get sneaky about it. Open the wine list, ask, "Do you have anything else like this you'd recommend?" and point to a price you're comfortable with. The table will think you just can't pronounce fancy bottles of Pessac-Léognan, but the waiter/sommelier will take the hint.

Reasons to Go BTG

Stop, drop the bottle list, and roll with glasses if:

➤ Everyone else is drinking cocktails.

➤ Everyone else is drinking beer.

➤ Everyone else is on a juice cleanse that prohibits alcohol but somehow does not prohibit eating three-fourths of a cheese plate they "just wanted a bite of."

➤ They have a bomb BTG list and you want to try them all.

➤ You've already had a bottle (*whooooops!*).

---

7. **Be wary of the second-cheapest bottle.** Restaurants are not dumb. They see you, out on a third date you can't believe you're having with someone you met off that new app, and they know you want to impress this person. You don't want to look cheap, so you order the second-cheapest bottle on the menu, in hopes that

it looks like you put some thought into it rather than beelining it to the bargain bottle. But let me tell you a little secret: The second-cheapest bottle on the menu can be the worst in value. **Restaurants will often price very cheap wines as the second-cheapest in order to cash in on the profit margin created by people's insecurity.** If you see wines you're familiar with at reasonable market rates, rest at ease. But if you see that grocery store wine you used to chug at $4 a bottle going for $10 a glass, give pause.

8. **Don't get hung up on pronunciations.** If you're scared, point at it. If you're brave, say whatever weird French shit you want, and you and the waiter can laugh about your horrible accent. This is key. Knowing that it's okay that you said it wrong, and laughing about it, takes the edge off the whole ordering process. After they tell you how it's actually pronounced, repeat it back so it sticks in your brain. Practice makes perfect!

Think Twice before Making It a Double

Love your bottle so much that it's empty before you've gotten through small bites? Before you motion to the waiter for another round of the same, take another gander at the wine list. Many wines are sold only in restaurants, so take advantage of this opportunity to try new things.

House Wine: Delicious Deal or Toxic Swill?

Many restaurants have house wines, affordable wines available by the glass, carafe, or sometimes by the bottle. The ambiguous title of "House Red" or "House White" doesn't instill much confidence, but that doesn't mean it's bad wine. Many restaurants feature rare finds or staff favorites as their house wines, or even have their own house wines made for them. It's best practice to ask your server about house wines rather than write them off.

Remember when buying and ordering wine used to stress you out? Crazy, right? Seems like only yesterday a trip to the wine shop made you feel more uneasy than public speaking, and you recoiled from wine lists like they were printed on paper made of poison oak. It was because you didn't have a game plan, but now you have the play-by-play for wine shops and restaurants. When you combine these strategies with your knowledge of what wines you like and how wines are made, getting yourself a good bottle becomes as effortless as Amazon Priming yourself shampoo. Well, except you do have to leave the house, but at least you don't have to take a paper bag for hyperventilating anymore. Buying and ordering wine is a piece of cake, but better because it's wine.

To-Drink List:

1. Try out a new wine shop, and make a point to chat.
2. Tell your nerves to get the fuck out of here, you're trying to buy wine!
3. Buy a bottle that is recommended to you because it's new, it's good, it's weird, or it's what the shopkeeper is drinking.
4. Volunteer to order the wine next time you're out to dinner.
5. High-five!

CHAPTER NINE

Hosting & Entertaining

This may come as a shock, but the true joy of wine isn't just drinking it. It's drinking it with loved ones. After all, what's the point of knowing all this stuff if you don't have anyone to talk about it with? In this chapter, I'm going to teach you how to take your skills from the bottle to the table so you can invite all your friends over and share all your wine with them. All right, not all of it. Let's not be hasty.

(Fact: You will get drunk and share all of it.)

If I was a rapper, half of my verses would be about how I'm the best host in the world. Bold, I know. I'm not even drunk and I'm this sure of myself. But that is because it's true. I'm a natural-born entertainer who also happens to be a perfectionist with an eye for color, composition, and empty glasses. And I got it all from my momma.

My mom, Gail, is one of the greatest hosts of all time, I daresay better than Martha and Gwyneth combined. Growing up, we were constantly entertaining: dinner parties with full table sets of vintage china, holiday parties with multiple trees dressed better than actresses going to the Oscars, "Thank fuckin' God the softball season is over" parties with more dips than any human should even know exist. She was singlehand-edly responsible for my slight bump in popularity in junior high after a string of birthday and Halloween parties that fea-tured seven-foot snack spreads and the biggest bounce houses available for rent. All with matching serving ware, mind you.

No matter the purpose of the party, my mom approached every event with the same amount of preparation, attention to detail, and focus on fun. There was always a theme and a color scheme, with food, bevvies, and a full six-disc CD changer to set the mood. Her infectious laugh rang from the kitchen, and every task was performed with a smile. And while I knew how much work went into these get-togethers at the Ross Residence, a guest would never know that it was anything more than the twist of my mother's wrist spiraling a stack of color-coordinated napkins on the corner of a table. My mother had a way of mak-ing sure no one ever had a want in the world. Everything was always taken care of before you knew it needed to be.

And *that* is what makes me a great host. It's not how clean my house is, or the music I play, or my charming personality. What makes me a great host is that there is never an empty glass. Whether we're eating dinner or chillin' on the couch or having an impromptu dance party, I'm sharing my wine, and my love of wine, with you.

And just like my mom, people think I just live my life this way. "Oh, all this wine? These glasses? This very specific cheese? Oh, I just had them *lying around*!"

No. Definitely not. Hosting takes time, effort, practice,

and some strategy. But by the end of this chapter, you'll feel ready to host everything from black-tie dinner parties to Chinese takeout on the couch with your best friends.

CALCULATING HOW MUCH WINE YOU NEED

If you've found yourself standing in front of a wall of wine trying to count how many people are coming to dinner and then cursing yourself because what is 750ml *really*, I feel you. You now know I can't do math, and I also can't be bothered to remember simple measurements like how many ounces are in 750ml. For the record, it's 25 point blah blah ounces.

If you were to remember that a standard bottle of wine has ~25 ounces, and that the suggested wine serving is 5 ounces, you could conclude that for every bottle of wine you get five glasses. You could then apply this to your total number of guests and buy accordingly. This is a logical and fine way of doing things, that I do not personally do.

First of all, five ounces is a joke. Saying you're going to just have five ounces of wine is the equivalent of claiming you're going to only have one piece of pizza when we know damn well you are down for two (or eight). Even if you did come across some straight-laced lunatic who was hung up on having exactly five ounces, you would need one of those portion control pour-tops reserved for stingy chain restaurants with ominous "house wines" they can't bear to give you a single drop extra of. And even if you decided to be diligent about your serving sizes, that would not stop someone like me from rolling up and destroying your portions with my heavy-handed pour I'm not even paying attention to because I'm yelling shitty jokes at someone across the room. No one wants five ounces. They want a goddamn glass of wine, a size that varies wildly depending on the scene.

Trust me, the five-glasses-per-bottle ratio will always leave you coming up short. There are too many variables, and you will end up looking either unprepared or Scrooge-like as you ration the last Syrah. Those are two of the most unbecoming looks as a host. Hosting is essentially (1) looking like you have your shit together and (2) being generous, things you should want in life regardless of how many movie nights you're trying to throw next summer.

My preferred ratio is four glasses per bottle, though a more accurate description would probably be, "four heavy pours and two swigs," or as they are known in my household, "four Ross pours and two Ross Tests." I like this ratio because it gives me the freedom to be rambunctious with my pours. Few things pleasure me quite like filling guests' glasses with the carefreeness of a chart-topping hip-hop artist popping Champagne in the club for their crew.

In a perfect world, I would have enough wine to fill every glass to the moon and back. Unfortunately, we live in a world where reality TV stars can become president, smoking weed is still a federal offense, and writers' signing contracts are nowhere near sport stars'. In other words, the world is not perfect, so it's important to estimate how many glasses you have per person.

For dinner parties, I generally allot two to three glasses per person. If I just got paid, I will buy one bottle of wine per person. If this sounds a little excessive, well, it is. But wine is my life, and sharing it brings me immense happiness. Plus, I'm a wine writer, and that brings with it a certain type of expectation. People come over to my house and they want to drink *everything*, so I need to be heavily stocked so I don't end up opening some Beaujolais cru I'm supposed to be aging for the next five years.

If I'm hosting a house party, though, there's no way I am buying one bottle per person. Gamay may run in my blood, but I am not made of bottles. I usually buy six to ten bottles, depending on the size of the party. I know that many partiers are going to be drinking my dope-ass wine and some are going to be drinking our stock of run-of-the-mill beers with equal enthusiasm, so no, not everyone gets a bottle to chug without a thought and then go play glow-in-the-dark bocce ball.

How many glasses of wine you are willing to serve each guest is up to you and your budget. I know I said you should be generous, but that doesn't mean you should be putting yourself in the pourhouse (HA, NAILED IT) to have some friends over. Be honest with yourself and what you're comfortable with. Plus, what are friends for if not for bringing more wine? Always ask guests to contribute. Tack it onto the end of the text, make it your new signature: "Please bring wine to share." People always want to contribute, and it takes some of the pressure off you. It also stops you from opening bottles, more bottles than you allocated for the event, or worse, drunkenly opening something you've been saving.

In conclusion, here is the only math I'll ever do:

Number of Guests × Number of Estimated Glasses Per Guest ÷ 4
= Number of Bottles Needed

TOOLS OF THE TRADE

I'm a very "jeans and a T-shirt" type of person. I like the finer things, no doubt, but I'm fairly no-frills about most things in life. I like good investments and things that are simple and useful, and the same goes for my wine tool kit. You wouldn't find any DIY wine charms, glitter-dipped Merlot glasses, or cowboy-boot bottle holders in my house. Here are the only things you really need to serve wine like a pro.

One-Size-Fits-All Stemware

Once upon a time, I had multiple sets of wine glasses. I had red-wine glasses, white-wine glasses, hell, I even had Champagne flutes. At twenty-six, I had become an adult. By twenty-seven, I had one red-wine glass, two white-wine glasses, and half a Champagne flute. Having different sets of glasses for different wines is a rich man's game, which if you are rich and can afford to continually replace all these different glasses as you and your friends inevitably break them, by all means, indulge your whims. I hope one day to be so lucky, but currently, I don't have the time, money, or energy to be worrying about where I'm going to get a matching vintage Pinot Noir glass now that my favorite Etsy seller has gotten a corporate job.

I'm all about having one standard glass that you serve everything in. Doesn't matter what it is, as long as it has a stem and you can drink wine out of it. You want glasses with stems because stemless glassware is only good for red wines (your hands warm up the wine while you drink out of them, so they suck for anything cold). My personal go-to is the Crate & Barrel Nattie Red Wine Glass. I like red-wine glasses as my standard glasses because they're a little bigger than white-wine glasses, and I like them from Crate & Barrel because they are always there and are $3.95, or $28 for a set of eight.

Pro tip: Ask for a set of your preferred wineglasses every year for whatever gift-receiving holiday you celebrate. Not *this* year, *every year.* As the year progresses and your glasses start dropping like flies, it's just a quick trip to your closet to keep your set complete.

Multiple (Double-Hinged) Corkscrews

Corkscrews are integral to the wine-drinking experience. There's something about the ritual of it, and that popping sound, that is just so exciting. And there are so many types. You've got those fancy machine ones your parents give each other for Christmas, the cheap grocery store ones that make opening a bottle of wine as easy as pulling an old nail out of a wall with a crappy hammer, and those plastic ones from hotels that make you understand why people try to open bottles with their shoes. My personal choice is the double-hinged corkscrew.

Relatively self-explanatory, the double-hinged corkscrew (also called a wine key) has an extra hinge for more power while pulling out the cork. It makes it a much smoother experience, and cuts down on having to use Hulk-like strength to pull the cork out.

For entertaining, you need at least two corkscrews available at all times, because everyone misplaces them. I am *still* looking for my favorite corkscrew I misplaced during a party three months ago! Having multiple corkscrews means you and your guests can be opening bottles and losing corkscrews all over the house, and still be able to serve more wine. And lose more corkscrews, because life is cruel and unrelenting.

Wine Stoppers

When you care about the wines you drink, you want to have stoppers to preserve them for later. *I know* that you think you're going to always finish your bottles once you open them. I thought that for a while, too. I also thought that I would never have big pores, and then one day, I woke up and was older, with legit pores, and wished I had put a stopper in that half-full bottle of Spanish Mourvèdre instead of leaving it out and ruining what could've made an excellent afternoon snack.

The cork you pull out of the bottle is great for this, but there's too many unknowns. What if you accidentally trash it? Or your cat has batted it off into the great void under your bed? Or it expanded and just won't fucking fit? Foil is fine for an emergency and for the illusion that it actually might help keep a wine fresh (it doesn't—it just keeps fruit flies at bay), but you can't be doing that regularly.

Decanters & Aerators

Like people, some wines need breathing room. Both old wines and new wines benefit from being decanted since they are bottled up, both literally and figuratively. Their flavors are tight and sharp because they've been confined to a small space. Imagine if you were stuck in a closet for three years. You would probably be pretty damn edgy when you got out and you'd need to walk, if not run and jump and do somersaults, in order to chill out and be yourself again. Same principle with wine. Decanting allows a wine to relax and become smoother as its volatile compounds, which may make it taste and smell pungent, "blow off" due to evaporation.

But what happens if you open a wine you didn't know needed to be decanted when everyone is already seated for dinner? This is why it's good to have an aerator. These handy handheld devices make it easy to quickly aerate wine as you pour it into your guests' glasses. Run the rest of the bottle through the aerator into the decanter, and pray you're the only one who notices it's on the acidic side (you probably will be; most people are happy just to be drinking at all).

When Should I Decant Wine?

Good question, with a two-part answer. The first part is very cut-and-dried: *Always decant wines that have been aging for long periods of time to separate sediment.* The second part is a little murky, because decanting mostly comes down to personal preference. If a wine tastes too acidic, too tannic, too high in alcohol, or too anything you're not digging straight out of the bottle, decant it for an hour and try it again. Some wines take less time for these qualities to blow off and their flavors open up, other wines take more. There is no exact formula for decanting. When buying wine, ask your retailer if they would recommend any decanting, and always trust your taste buds.

Plasticware

I'm not a fan of drinking out of plastic. Something about it always takes me back to Solo cups and bad choices. But I am grown enough to put these feelings aside and recognize their necessity when it comes to drinking outside. Whether it's a picnic at the park or just hanging on your porch, plastic glasses will ensure that your wineglasses won't be kicked, stepped on, or otherwise destroyed. Sure, you have that extra set of wineglasses for these sorts of accidents, but picking glass out of your lawn isn't anyone's idea of fun. Unless it's a small group of people you trust, and there are plenty of tables around, always go plastic for outdoor hang sessions.

An Ice Bucket, I Guess

I'm not that into ice buckets. They tend to make wines too cold, but I'd be lying if I didn't say they weren't helpful when entertaining so you're not hopping up from the table every forty-two seconds. Use at your discretion, and keep your eyes (mouth) on the wine. If it starts tasting one-noted because it's so cold, take it out of the bucket to warm up for a bit. The only thing that needs to be served that cold is crappy Pinot Grigio.

Wine Away

I don't know how I am not paid by this company, considering how often I tell people about them, but this is not sponsored content. Wine Away is a citrus-based spray that is safe on most fabrics, and has saved my entire closet, my sheets, and a fair share of rugs from being annihilated by wine. I keep a bottle in my bathroom so I look considerate to guests, but it's really because I use it daily. It's simple to use: Just spray immediately after your spill. Many times it will disappear like magic right in front of your eyes. Just don't use Wine Away on dry-clean-only items. It doesn't do anything to the clothes, but it really pisses off dry cleaners.

Spit Bucket (Optional)

As a wine writer, there are days when I am tasting dozens of wines before nightfall and don't want to be hungover by dinner, so a spit bucket comes in handy. This isn't an essential accessory to have, but you may need one if you decide to host a more formal wine tasting at your house.

PAIRING FOOD & WINE

There isn't a good thing in this world that doesn't rely on balance. From nature to music to relationships, it's all about harmony between different elements. When pairing food and wine, that is exactly what you're doing—finding components that complement and play off each other to create an entirely new and delicious experience that neither the dish nor the glass could be on its own. It's enchanting, like something you put together in Potions class at Hogwarts to charm the pants off your guests.

Much like potions (or pimpin'), pairing ain't easy. Pairing takes a bit of knowledge, some consideration, and a lot of trial and error. But not only does practice make perfect, it makes for a great excuse to eat, drink, and be merry. Here's everything you need to know to start practicing your wine pairing skills tonight.

For Starters

You need to know what you're eating. The flavors of the dish are what influence your wine choices; think of them as the beats that your wine rhymes on top of. Doesn't matter how great a flow is if it's not on beat. Is your meal rich and buttery? Or light and salty? Spicy? Earthy? Sweet? Greasy, raunchy goodness? Identifying the dominant flavors and characteristics of your meal is half the work. Once you know the main elements of the dish, you then know what elements you need in a wine to balance and complement it.

The Balancing Act

I don't know much about cooking. At the time I am writing this, I've cooked approximately a dozen times in my whole life. But I've watched a lot of *Top Chef*, and if there's anything that the goddess Padma, bald eagle Tom, and my pretend mentor Gail have taught me, it's that a great dish has a balance of fat, acid, salt, and sweet. Those are the same qualities you're looking for to find an equilibrium between what you're eating and what you're drinking.

Fatty Foods

I wish there was a less crude classification for these foods, one that feels less like I'm shaming them and more like I'm celebrating the joy cheeseburgers bring into my life, but alas. The "Fatty Foods" category covers all meat, as well as dishes featuring butter or cream sauces. I've broken this down by two categories, lighter and darker, based on the physical color of the dishes. It's the easiest way for me to remember it, and hopefully for you, too. Acidic wines pair well with lighter dishes like salmon, chicken, pork, and dishes with butter or cream sauces. The acid cuts through the fat, leaving your mouth feeling refreshed and ready for another bite. Tannic wines pair well with darker fatty foods like steak, lamb, and all that other red meat carnivore stuff. While tannins dry up and neutralize some of the fat's richness, the richness of the fat also keeps your mouth from drying up like the Sahara from high tannin levels.

PRACTICE WITH:

Grilled Salmon & Pinot Noir
Steak & Cabernet Sauvignon
Roast Chicken & Grüner Veltliner
AVOID AT ALL COSTS: *Sweet wines like off-dry Rieslings or Chenin Blancs, and dessert wines like Port*

Fishes Are Delicious with . . . Red Wine?

You bet. Red wine is *not* just for meat, and white wine is *not* just for fish. Both red wines and white wines (and rosés and oranges, too) have such broad spectrums of characteristics that living by this rule would rule out half of the exciting and unexpected pairings that are possible.

Try: Beaujolais with oysters, pork chops with orange Pinot Gris, oaked Chardonnay with steak

Acidic Foods

You'd think you'd want something sweet to balance out acidic foods, but it's actually better to pair with a wine that adds *more* acid. Counterintuitive, I know. But bright dishes featuring citrus, tomatoes, and salad dressings like vinaigrette will crush wines with less acidity than the dish itself, leaving the wine lifeless and tasting dull in comparison.

PRACTICE WITH:

Pasta with Fresh Tomato Sauce & Sangiovese
Citrus Salad & Txakoli
Panzanella & Vermentino
AVOID AT ALL COSTS: *Low-acidity wines*

Salty Foods

Salty foods like oysters, parmesan, or anything fried do well with acidic wines. The saltiness of the dish is tempered by the tartness of the acid, and by the same token, the salt of the dish brings down the sour flavor of the wine. If you want to throw your salt tooth a party, pop some sparkling wine. The number one palate cleanser recommended by wine professionals, sparkling wines scrub salt off your palate and make you hungry, and thirsty, for more. If you have a sweet tooth, pair your salty dish with a sweeter wine for a contrast as delightful as dipping French fries in milk shakes.

PRACTICE WITH:

Fried Chicken & Champagne
Chinese Food & Chenin Blanc
Bleu Cheese & Sauternes
AVOID AT ALL COSTS: *Tannic wines*

Sweet Foods

There are two schools of thought on sweet foods. Some people treat them like acidic foods, insisting you need a wine that is sweeter than the dish or you run the risk of the wine tasting blasé. I'm guessing those people have serious sweet teeth, though, because I'm from the school that thinks pairing sweet wines with sweet foods is overkill. I prefer wines that have hints of sweetness, but aren't lighter and sweeter than the dessert.

Chocolate Cake & Port
Apple Pie & Vouvray Moelleux
Anything & Amaro
AVOID AT ALL COSTS: *Dry wines*

Spicy Foods

Of all the dumb, baseless urban legends out there, my least favorites are the one where a bunch of spiders hatch from a woman's face, and the one about how you can't drink wine with spicy
foods. Preposterous! But I understand the origin of this myth,
unlike the Chupacabra. Pairing wine with spicy foods is hard,
because spice is not a flavor but a feeling, and alcohol intensifies
that sensation. But trust me, sweet and off-dry white wines as
well as low-alcohol, fruity, chilled red wines will tame the flame.

PRACTICE WITH:

Fish Tacos & Riesling
Thai Green Curry & Gamay
Pork Vindaloo & Gewürztraminer
AVOID AT ALL COSTS: *High-alcohol wines, tannic wines,*
and oaked wines

Earthy Foods & Fruity Foods, Respectively

Earthy foods, like mushrooms and lentils, and dishes with fruit
or heavy fruit components like a glaze or a sauce, are easy.
They just want to hang out with likewine'ed bottles.

PRACTICE WITH:

Mushrooms & Nebbiolo
Roasted Pork with Apples & Viognier

And Remember . . .

Sometimes you're in a hurry or under pressure and the last thing you have time for is contemplating low-alcohol wines versus high-alcohol wines. Here are some quick tips to keep in your back pocket for when you just need a good pairing.

Like Goes with Like. Wines and foods that are similar in weight and/or complexity pair well. Light-bodied wines go with lean meals; full-bodied wines go with rich meals. Complex wines with multiple layers of flavor should be paired with equally intricate meals, and straightforward wines should be served with simple meals. An elaborate Syrah isn't going to be enhanced by a salami sandwich you're eating over the sink, nor will a straightforward Pinot Grigio do much for a much-slaved-over coq au vin.

Where It Grows, It Goes. Whatever country's cuisine you're cookin', there is a good chance their wine will pair well with it. Italian wines with Italian food, New Zealand wine with New Zealand cheese, Oregon wine with a *Portlandia* marathon. This isn't foolproof, though—a big, tannic red isn't going to go with paella just because it's from Spain.

Tannins Never Go with Bitter. EVER. Tannic wines make bitter foods unbearable to eat. Yes, this includes red wine and chocolate. That's not real. That's a sexy lie some marketing person made up to sell more lube.

Practically Unpairable

These foods are the edible equivalent of that one friend you keep trying to set up on dates. You love them, they're great, but they're never going to go for you matching them up. Unlike your friend (hopefully!), what makes these foods so difficult is that they all contain organic sulfur compounds. Add a bit of wine and you've got a mouth full of rotten eggs.

➤ Brussels Sprouts, Asparagus, Broccoli, Cauliflower

THE MOST IMPORTANT THING TO PAIR WITH

Above all else, at the end of the day, the most important thing you need to pair your food and wine with is your mouth.

Trying established pairings that consider fats and acids and all that jazz gets you in the habit of thinking and tasting how food and wine work together, but you should try everything. Try pairing your favorite wines with your favorite dishes. Try pairing wines with foods that you just have a feeling will be good together. Try pairing wines you just happen to have with whatever you just happen to be eating. Successful food and wine pairings don't happen because ACID + ACID FOREVER was carved into the wall of an ancient cellar in

France and taken as gospel. Successful food and wine pairings happen because of experimentation.

By "successful," I mean successful for you. Beyond rules and recommendations and even rational thought, what matters is finding combinations *you* think are delicious. Hopefully, you share them and everyone else thinks they're delicious, too, but if not, whatever. Then you know what you're serving next Friday when you have the house all to yourself.

COURSING WINES WITH DINNER

"Coursing wines" is when you serve specific wines in order, to pair with specific dishes. If you've ever had a tasting menu, you've probably seen that there is almost always a wine-pairing option. Even if you're not serving up a flow of small plates, you can still course your wines. You don't have to—it's much simpler to buy stuff you like and throw it on the table—but it can add an exciting element to your next gathering. Plus, it solidifies your new place as the "wine friend," which we all know is the real reason you bought this book.

How to Impress as a Guest

Sooo, you're not hosting. But you do love wine! Now what? Be the best goddamn guest ever hosted, that's what. Here's how:

➤ **Never ask if you should bring wine. *Always bring wine.***

➤ **Ask your host if there is a specific type of wine they would like you to get to pair with the meal, because you are thoughtful like that.**

➤ **If they don't have a specific wine in mind, ask what they're cooking so you can try to pair something yourself, or bring a versatile and food-friendly wine like [wait for it] Gamay or Riesling.**

➤ **If your budget allows, bring two bottles of wine. The one the host requested (or you picked out) and one you want to share with everyone because you love it (and them) so much.**

➤ **Aside from always bringing wine because it's the right thing to do, always bring wine because you cannot assume that an event is going to have wine you like. It's better to bring something you enjoy and open it rather than get there and get sick on gas station Shiraz.**

Coursing your wines with dinner is one of the ultimate curations. Think of it like putting together a playlist. A good playlist takes its listeners on a journey. The first song sets up the overall vibe, the next section steadily increases in tempo leading up to the middle, which should act as the peak of the playlist, followed by a gradual, easy comedown. Each song complements the one before it as well as the one after, bridging moods to produce an overall experience.

Same thing with wine! All you need is your menu and your newfound food-pairing knowledge to get started. Let's do this.

Wines should always be served lightest to heaviest because as you eat and drink, your palate becomes fatigued, making it harder to pick up on subtler flavors. You don't want to have a guest walk in and overwhelm their palate with a mug of port before they've even had a nosh. Think about your wine courses the same way you would think about food courses. Appetizers are usually on the lighter side, unless you're stoned at a chain restaurant and *have* to have a Blooming Onion. But since you're not running an Outback out of your basement, remember appetizers are light. They are followed by increasingly substantial courses, like salad, soup, mains, desserts.

It's easy to want to base "lightest to heaviest" on color, but it should be based on body. Red will almost always be your entrée wine unless you're serving a delicate fish, but sparkling wines, white wines, rosé wines, and orange wines are all interchangeable for everything leading up to that, based on their weight.

But choose wines that pair with your dishes. It's easy to get caught up in selecting the light- to full-bodied choices and forget all about the food. But complementing your dishes is a big part of why you're doing this, so bring your menu along with you when you go shopping for selections.

Have a light arrival wine. You know in the movies

when you see a party at a mansion and there's a butler right inside the door with a tray of full Champagne flutes? Keep that in mind as you play host. You don't need to get a tux and serve up Krug, but the arrival wine should be light, easy, and acidic to get everyone's mouths watering and ready to eat. Also note that this wine should not be the highlight of the evening. If your friends are anything like mine, you will tell them five, and half of them will show up at six and be all sorts of butthurt that they missed out on something special you served an hour ago. (Serves them right, honestly. There is nothing I hate more than lateness, but a good host is gracious and shouldn't hold grudges. I do, but you know what they always say: "Do as I say not as I begrudge.")

Don't repeat flavors. You wouldn't have two cucumber soups on a menu, or make half your playlist the Rolling Stones' *Let It Bleed*. There are always exceptions, like if your dinner's theme is all about different variations on a single ingredient, or if you're hosting my dream dinner of "Gamay Five Ways." But generally, you want to vary the flavors. This doesn't mean you can't serve multiple sparkling wines, or even two Chardonnays—just make sure they are different enough to make, well, a difference!

Keep bottles stocked for provisional, between-course, and rambunctious drinking. No matter how well you course things and try to keep people on track, there's no stopping guests from drinking when they want to drink. Pick something that is (1) light enough that you could sneak a glass between small bites and salads without disrupting your courses, (2) food-friendly enough that you won't mind if it makes its way onto the table along with your main course, and (3) inexpensive enough that you won't mind if your college buddy decides to throw back a couple bottles for dessert.

Don't Get Too Complicated. This is a mistake I often make. My husband will choose the menu, and I will pore over the ingredients, asking a million questions: Is rosemary the dominant flavor? Are all these leeks going in the soup? What is the orange for? I research the recipes and catch myself trying to find "the right" bottles, obsessed with highlighting and nuancing and creating this whole experience that no one is thinking about nearly as intensely as I am. Your guests will appreciate the meal, whether or not the Sancerre really ties the fennel dish together, so skip the stress and just have fun.

My Ideal Coursing

If I were to close my eyes and picture the dinner party I would put together this very afternoon for you, this is what it would be.

Arrival Wine: Dry Rosé
Provisional Wine: Beaujolais-Villages
Appetizers: Charcuterie and Brut Sparkling
Salad: Little Gems with my grandmother's vinaigrette and Vinho Verde
Soup: Tomato Soup and Barbera d'Alba
Main: Roast Chicken and Beaujolais Morgon
Dessert: Nothing but some fancy-ass Sherry

PAIRING YOUR WINE WITH MUSIC

Before I wrote about wine, I wrote about music. Never professionally, aside from a handful of paychecks from *Pitchfork*, but I wrote about it for the same reasons I write about wine. Music, like wine, can transport you. You can be minding your own business, living your life, and then one of *those* songs comes on. Suddenly, you're somewhere else, like your old best friend's living room after the beach that one day, when the sun came in the windows just *so* and illuminated it in a golden glow as you danced on the couch and laughed until you cried, all salty and smelling of sunscreen. Music makes you feel something, often a lot of things! And together, music and wine have the power to shape a party.

This isn't just me being a weirdo that can't separate the things that I love. It's science. There have been a number of studies that indicate that music can change how you taste a wine. In 2010, Heriot-Watt University published a study that concluded, "Results reported here indicate that independent groups' ratings of the taste of the wine reflected the emotional connotations of the background music played while they drank it. These results indicate that the symbolic function of auditory stimuli (in this case music) may influence perception in other modalities (in this case gustation)." In other words, the wine will take on whatever characteristics you're hearing in the song. If it's a brooding folk album that makes you think of your family cabin, you may taste a woodsy depth in your glass, just like you may feel a tinge of lemonade acidity while listening to surf rock.

A few years ago, I attended a blind tasting at a winery that focused on the effects of music on wine. The tasting was a mix of winery guests and industry professionals, wine merchants and beverage directors. We were all blindfolded, and different wines were served at the same temperature in black glasses, so there was no way to cheat. Each wine was served with a different song, and we would go around the room debating on what wine we were being served.

The effect of the music was most apparent in the middle of the tasting. One glass was served with a super-poppy song. One glass was served with a Fleet Foxes song. One glass was served with a slow, moody song. The guesses for each song ranged wildly. Everyone associated the wine we drank during the poppy song with bright, white wines. Fleet Foxes provoked discussions of medium-bodied wines both red and white, and the moody song had everyone going very dark in their guesses.

No one guessed Zinfandel.

And no one guessed that it was Zinfandel in *all three glasses.*

Now picture yourself as the badass host that you are. You've picked up a few bottles of your new favorite wine to share with your friends tonight. You all have similar taste and this is right up their alley, a bright, spunky, and fruity red that is even good when chilled. You're one hundred percent confident it's going to be the new crew go-to, the wine of the summer. "Everyone is going to think it's Gamay, boy, will I have them fooled! HA HAAAA!" you laugh triumphantly to yourself. This will be your moment. Your wine!

You uncork the bottle, pour, and eagerly watch them

drink it, like you're forcing them to watch your favorite TV show and keep looking over to see if they're laughing. But they're not laughing. And the wine is "Good."

Good?! This was supposed to be their new favorite wine! How are you friends with these people? They're crazy. You try it yourself, incredulous, and realize . . . they're right. It's not fantastic. It's not the best thing since the original seasons of *Arrested Development*. It's just, *fine*.

There are many reasons why a wine's taste could vary from one bottle to another, even in the same vintage. But maybe—just maybe—it tastes different because Bright Eyes came on shuffle. Everyone groaned the groan of the emo generation and told you to turn that shit off, but you didn't. You let a slow bummer of a song play as you encouraged everyone to tip their glasses of fun, zippy wine to their frowning lips. Considering Fleet Foxes can make Zinfandel taste like Viognier, it isn't that far-fetched to think that Bright Eyes may have blown your bottle.

Even if that scenario is a little far-fetched, pairing music with your wine is still a good idea, if only to save the mood of your party from shuffle disasters. Whether you're hand-picking a playlist, throwing on some records, or selecting a Spotify radio station, choose music that enhances your wine's flavors and elevates your get-together's vibes. Here's how I do it.

Know the vibe. What kind of get-together is this? Dinner party or pajama party? Birthday bash or backyard barbeque? Date night or *daaaaate* night? Hopefully, you know why people are coming over to your house; if not, definitely figure that out first.

Buy wines based on that vibe. You've got this already.

Evaluate wines' body and acidity. Think about a wine's body as sweaters and its acidity as energy. The more sweaters you're wearing, the more you want to get cozy, but the more energy you have, the more you want to dance. The lighter and more acidic the wines are, the more upbeat the jams. It accentuates their brightness and drinkability, and enhances tart fruit and citrus notes. The heavier and richer the wines are, the more chill and down-tempo the music. It complements their warmth and weight, as well as spice and sweetness.

Look outside. Take the weather and the season into consideration. Spring, summer, and sunshine inspire very different music choices than fall, winter, and rain. For me, the warmer months are all about surf rock, poppy oldies, jangly garage bands, bossa nova, hip-hop, and exotica. When it's colder, I lean toward folk rock, acoustics, evocative vocals, cool jazz, and Christmas music. And still exotica, which throws everyone off. Which brings me to my next point.

Listen to what you want to listen to. I listen to exotica year-round, and I don't give a damn if someone may find tiki lounge or the occasional tropical bird call unseasonal.

I then take all of these factors into consideration and make an educated selection of music that promotes the vibe of the get-together, complements the wine, and is seasonal. Or I put on Monster Rally, and there's nothing anyone can do about it.

The Hit List

You may not have gathered this yet, but I'm pretty neurotic, especially about wine, music, and keeping my house superclean. But sometimes I don't have time to curate our hang sesh with a custom DJ set and coursed wines. Here are my split-second decision seasonal go-tos.

Spring: Rosé & Drake
Summer: Vinho Verde & the Ventures
Fall: Cabernet Franc & Real Estate
Winter: Syrah & Dave Brubeck
365: Gamay & Martin Denny

Hosting isn't about having the perfect pairings. It isn't about having specific glassware, or a well-crafted playlist. Those things are nice, but hosting always comes back to being generous. I don't mean with money spent, or even bottles opened; it's about being generous with yourself. All it takes to be the best host ever is kindness and good conversation over a glass of wine you can't wait to share with your guests. (Cheese doesn't hurt, though.)

To-Drink List:

1. Pair wine with dinner using your new pairing tips. Get a good idea of what you're looking for: red or white, dry

or off-dry, acidic or fruity. When you go into the wine shop, instead of asking for what's new, ask for a dry, acidic white to pair with your grilled chicken, or whatever it is you're cooking. Extra Challenge: Try pairing with wines you already have in your house. Maybe this is your big chance to use that White Zin that's been in the fridge since last New Year's! (Just kidding. That needs to go in the trash immediately.)

2. Experience how much music affects the taste of wine by pouring yourself a glass, and sip on it, eyes closed, while listening to three contrasting songs. If you want to really get into it, write down how these songs affected your mood as well as how the wine tastes. Don't listen to anything too sad, though—I don't need you falling down a wine hole and texting ex-lovers and watching sappy period pieces all night.

3. Get yourself a double-hinged corkscrew. Maybe even get two if you just got paid. Pulltap makes great ones. They are $10 on Amazon and will make opening wine infinitely less shitty.

4. Host a little something at your house. Plan some pairings for your favorite wines, maybe put together some music if you have time. Get your guests talking about wine by telling them why you chose the wines you did, and what you love about them, and ask your guests what they think about them. Do they know how to taste wine? Maybe you can give them a few tips. Who knows, you may teach one of them to chew their wine and change their goddamn life.

CHAPTER TEN

Drinking Wine in the Real World

Not all wine consumption happens civilly over dining tables or in a winery's tasting room, belly-to-the-bar. Sometimes you're taking a few bottles with you into the great outdoors. Sometimes you're up for a promotion when your boss drags you out for happy hour. Sometimes you're at Grandma's for Easter and you're one bad glass of Merlot away from mauling your Libertarian cousin. All likely scenarios, and all less controllable than opening a Chianti from the comforts of your couch. Whether you're drinking in public or accidentally hosting a wine-fueled heart-to-heart with friends, this chapter will help you navigate life with glass in hand.

HOW TO DRINK WINE ANYWHERE

I don't believe that wine is only meant for dinner tables. The smell of it can take you back to dewy, redwood forest mornings;

a taste and you're midair off the diving board before cannon-balling into your childhood pool, mother's roses in bloom. Wine takes you overseas, inspires overtures, evokes orchestras. It's that one Fourth of July, that one ski lodge, that one night their hand grazed yours. How could you possibly confine wine to a glass on the right, just above the butter knife? There are plenty of state laws that disagree with me, but I believe that wine is for everywhere, because it captures everything.

Well, not "everywhere." It's not for the driver's seats of vehicles or heavy machinery, not for job interviews or court appearances, not for chilling on the couch with that friend you sometimes sleep with and regret, and definitely not for school. You have to use your head about these things, people! The last thing we responsible, irreverent drinkers need is some dummy chugging a case of wine on the corner of Holly-wood and Vine with this book in their jacket pocket like its *Catcher in the Rye* for alcoholics. Let this paragraph serve as a disclaimer, and let it be known I am not accountable for any of the shit you do. God speed, young ruffs.

But seriously, think of all the times you've sat back and thought to yourself, "A glass of wine would be really great right now." At that last-minute Sunday picnic, or atop the vista you spent all day backpacking, or while waiting in line for Splash Mountain. These are only a handful of the situations that would benefit greatly from wine, not to mention all the times you had to sit through a movie you didn't even want to see at the theater or those blissed-out, after-work, summer evening strolls. You don't need wine to enjoy these things. But I'm not going to pretend that wine doesn't go well with those things. And with a little preparation, you can drink anywhere.

On the Street

Drinking in public is considered a crime in many states, which is a bummer since I consider it more of a hobby. I understand that the point of these laws is to keep communities safe, and am definitely not encouraging any loaded rabble-rousing. B*uuu*t I also understand that sometimes it's summertime. And the livin' is easy. And the crew is meeting at your house before walking to the Cool Local Art & Music Festival. And it would be pretty nice to sip on a crisp rosé as you make your way down the handful of blocks before getting to the festival where you're probably going to end up with an overpriced Bud Light because the only wine there is Malbec and it's 96 degrees out.

Travel coffee cups with lids are perfect for transporting any wine, and green plastic twenty-ounce bottles for soda work fantastically for white wine. And there're always flasks, but personally I feel those are better suited for going to bars or concerts where you can get a glass to pour it out into.

At a Picnic

It's finally sunny out! Or maybe more appropriately, it's finally not a billion degrees out! It'd be a crime not to take advantage of such a fortunate forecast. Why drink inside when all you have to do is find some grass to unfurl your multipurpose Mexican blanket on, and voilà! A picnic!

For picnics, you want to bring light wines that can be thrown in an ice chest and won't taste totally awful if they don't make it back in said ice chest. Wines like Vinho Verde,

Grüner Veltliner, Txakoli, Vinho Verde, Gamay, Schiava, and Zweigelt are all bright, acidic, and easy. You can even throw some cubes in them if you need to. No one is interested in drinking a thick-ass Petite Sirah under the high afternoon sun. Overall big-bodied, heavy wines are not a good look for outdoor day-drinking and should be avoided.

Keep things copacetic and concealed by pouring wine into thermoses. With sizes up to two liters, thermoses can be used for quaint dates or to bring the freakin' party. Just don't bring it too hard because, ya know, we're responsible here. And I'm sure there is a kid with a piñata party somewhere nearby and you don't want to be *that* asshole.

Your Ass Is Glass

Glass containers in many public spaces are simply not allowed—and if you're caught possessing one, you may face a misdemeanor offense. Check out your area's laws against glass containers before taking any into public spaces.

At the Beach

My beach vibe has always been to make kalimotxos (kali-mo-cho), the red wine and Coca-Cola delicacy of my people on my mother's side, the Basques. If this sounds crazy to you, well, it's crazy to me that you haven't tried it! It's delicious! Kalimotxos are a great way to jazz up shit wine, although I personally don't encourage anyone to use any wine that is too sugary. The resulting hangover is usually Level "Why Did I Have Those Last Four Margaritas?"

Before you hit the sand, mix equal parts red wine and Coca-Cola in vessel of choice. I prefer to do this in twenty-ounce Coca-Cola bottles, with a ratio of two parts wine to one-part cola, but that's just me. The best wine for kalimotxos is whatever red wine you have, but ideally they are fruit-forward. Wines like Garnacha, Shiraz, Zinfandel, or Cabernet are all good choices. Grab some ice, your SPF, and you're ready to go.

Hit the Can

When it comes to portable wine for drinking solo or in small groups, nothing beats canned wines. Throw 'em in your bag for picnics, the beach, the movies, Sunday's softball game, or for the friend's birthday that you know is going to be a whiskey fest.

Places with Mad Security

On the one hand I want to say, "Dude, you're not getting wine into a Dodgers game. Trust me." But on the other hand I want to say, "Dude, I have totally gotten wine into a Dodgers game!" It did involve me slitting the lining of a vintage bag and using fashion tape to adhere it back together, but I did it. Once. And goddamn did it feel great not to spend $18 on a shitty beer! But I'm not into the idea of telling you to destroy your property, so here are some other options.

When it comes to festivals, sports games, and other events where you're being patted down and your bags are being rummaged, sneaking wine in isn't easy. But if they allow outside sealed beverages, you can get real sneaky. I'm going to use the example of white wine and green-tinted soda bottles, although it can be used for any plastic bottles. For every bottle you want to sneak in, you need one extra bottle. Open one bottle per usual, and use a funnel (unless you're extremely skilled) to pour the white wine of your choice into the bottle. Take the second bottle and DO NOT OPEN IT. Instead, use a box cutter to cut into the bottle in the space of air between the soda and the top. Cut around the bottle, so you are left with just the fully capped top portion. Put it in a pot of boiling water for a few minutes, and the fully sealed cap will come right off. You can then twist that cap onto your wine soda bottle, and it looks and acts just like an unopened bottle. Use extra soda for spritzers while you're scheming.

You can also do this with bright red wines and juice bottles.

OR SO I'VE HEARD.

FROM FRIENDS.

OF FRIENDS.

Think inside the Box

Boxed wine is not just for grandmas. These days, there are legit bougie boxed wines, like geeky-good wines! Check for them at your local shop. Boxed wine is great for any large gathering. Each box has multiple liters, so they're more economical than buying bottles, and they stay fresher longer.

Out in the Wild

While a water bottle full of scotch is always a necessity in the back country, it's also nice to bring some wine. I recommend reds so you don't have to worry about them being supercold, but as always, you do you.

If you're car camping, or as I call it, Girl Scouting, you don't have to worry about how you're transporting the wine to your campground, because it's not like you're lugging shit up a mountain on your back. You're pulling your RAV4 into a parking spot. While you can bring as many bottles as your heart desires (car has room for), I still like to recommend boxed wines for these occasions. Boxed wine has more wine, takes up less space, and creates a lot less trash.

If you're backpacking—now that is another story. I've backpacked with wine twice. Not because I didn't bring wine on my other backpacking trips, but because those were the only two times I've gone backpacking aside from trekking from classroom to classroom in the halls of Upland High.

The first time I went backpacking, it was a fifty-mile, seven-day loop trip through Yosemite. This sounds extreme for an amateur with an intense fear of heights, but it was a group led by a ranger and we didn't have to carry equipment or food supplies. It was extremely fun, and I only had one serious panic attack while scaling down a rock face! I highly suggest it. While I was definitely one of the more inexperienced backpackers on the trip, I was the wine expert, as proven by the fact that I had two bottles of it every night and everyone else was stuck sucking apple juice and rationing hot whiskey. So how the hell did I lug around a case of wine? I didn't. I had mules do it for me.

If you're going on a trip that has permanent camps, check ahead with the base camp to see if they do mule-packing. It was $5 a bottle to have my wine delivered to the camps, and worth every penny to know they were waiting for me at the top of thirty-nine suicidal switchbacks. (And to see the look on this one winesplaining asshole's face who had been condescendingly quizzing me on his favorite Burgundies that day. Because if you don't know five random producers some old white dude has in his cellar in Michigan, you know nothing about wine, by the way.)

The second time I went backpacking, I was told that it was going to be "really easy." We were just going to be "walking along the river" and I should "bring the dogs." My dogs are Pomeranians, one of which ended up having to be carried for most of the hike because we were climbing straight up 3,500 feet, and I couldn't carry him because I had brought four bottles of wine because I had been under the impression the hike was "seriously not a big deal." Lesson learned: Trust no one and NEVER take bottles of wine backpacking. Shit is heavy and will ruin your hips, back, and life.

Instead of bottles, take bagged wine. This is as easy as grabbing a boxed wine and pulling the bag out, or buying a portable and collapsible plastic wine bag, options online.

Cool It!

Drinking wine in the great outdoors means you don't have the convenience of throwing a wine in the fridge, but that doesn't mean you have to drink hot wine. If you're close to water, drop the temperature by taking your wines for a dip. Secure bags or bottles in rivers or lakes for a quick chill, and always watch your labels! If left for too long, they will start to come off and end up downstream. Litterbugs are second only to bedbugs on my list of "Worst Fucking Bugs Ev." If you're not near water, you can also keep wines cool by burying them.

Busted

Have I been caught drinking where I shouldn't have been? Yes. Once. Which is astonishing considering all the years I spent drinking rum on the sand in San Clemente, running around the streets of Echo Park with cans of Tecate, and that one time I was chugging wine out of the bottle on Sunset Boulevard outside Origami Vinyl during a show I threw. It all started when I was reading on the beach. Maybe it started with the kalimotxos out of red cups. Doesn't matter how it started. Myself, my husband, Ben, and our friends Max and Bre were all sitting on a blanket, quietly reading, and I decided to enhance this very relaxing afternoon by sipping on some 'motxos.

Our reverie was interrupted by a large, rowdy group of preteens. They were playing loud music, kicking sand, and tossing dozens of single-serving bags of Cheetos into the wind. First of all, they invented party-size bags for this exact scenario. Second, no grade-school child, let alone like ten of them, should be consuming so many bags of Cheetos that a nearby stranger now feels they fully understand the cause of the childhood obesity epidemic. And third, THERE WAS A TRASH CAN RIGHT THERE! In between chapters, I stomped around picking up their litter and throwing it away while also properly throwing them nasty side-eyes because I am passive-aggressive as hell.

Out of nowhere, eight Malibu PD dune buggies pull up. One even had two officers, holding each other like a couple atop a horse trotting along the surf for an engagement photo. Their high-velocity entrance spoke volumes: They were going full throttle after criminals, which were, in my mind, fat kids who litter. "They must have seen my one-woman beach cleanup," I thought, smiling smugly and congratulating myself on my dedication to the environment. "There are the perpetrators, officers!" was almost out of my mouth before I realized the nine officers were surrounding me and one was asking, "Ma'am, what are you drinking?"

"Ma'am"?! Seriously? I told him I was drinking Cherry Coke, which he responded to by putting an alcohol-detecting police tampon* in my cup, which declared that it was not Cherry Coke. One of his badge buddies started rifling through our ice chest, while Ben sat quietly on a freshly packed bowl and Max began taking the rap for Bre. "They've got glass!" the officer announced, holding up a bottle of $2 Quail Oak. It all went downhill from there. I started chugging my very full cup, they started threatening me with misdemeanors; they asked for my information, I asked them if being a chill adult who is into literature and shitty wine was actually a crime because I was pretty damn sure that leaving behind enough snack trash to fill an elementary school lunchroom's garbage can was. After some back and forth, the cop decided not to give me a misdemeanor because in his words, "I'm cool and not an asshole." I was handed a $300 ticket for literally "drinking red wine and cola in a red cup on the beach." He and the other eight useless officers who had just been standing there jumped back on their dune buggies. We were left in the dust with the children, who continued to eat chips and contribute to five trillion pieces of trash in the ocean.

Moral of the story is, no good deed in beach cleanup goes unpunished.

In addition to teaching me never to use red cups again, I learned some other important things about what to do when you get busted for drinking.

---

* Not a real tampon but sure as hell looked like one. Maybe it was a real tampon. One of the great mysteries of our (my) time.

1. While I don't recommend telling the cops, unprompted, you are drinking alcohol, if they do ask you, be honest.
2. Tell them you'll toss it.
3. If they do write you a ticket, just take it and do so gracefully. You took the ride, and sometimes you've got to take the ticket with it.

KEEPING YOUR SHIT TOGETHER AT FAMILY FUNCTIONS

Family. They're stressful for everyone, even if you love the hell out of those assholes you share blood with. Given there is so much history between you all, there is bound to be some baggage, not to mention conflicting political views, conversations regarding your social media that you didn't realize your aunts were keeping up on, or being harassed about when you're going to finally get married (and then finally getting married and then being harassed about why you're not inviting your great-uncle Lenny who you've seen maybe five times in the last twenty years, although you cannot personally recall any of those five times, let alone remember who the fuck that is).

In case you couldn't guess, I come from a very large, very tight-knit family. On my father's side, there are twenty-five of us in the immediate family, not counting my cousins' partners or their children. That number starts to push forty, and as you can imagine, family functions are not quaint get-togethers. They are full-blown parties, full of full-blown personalities who admittedly I have not always gotten along with, no thanks to my own full-blown personality (or my adolescent habit of writing scathing and sarcastic essays online that got me more or less disowned multiple times). These days we are a big happy family, but that doesn't mean that drinking with them doesn't come with its perils, perils that over the years I have come to conquer like an Olympic hurdler. Here's how to enjoy wine with your family without getting into a fight about immigration and threatening to bring back the People's Elbow* on your aunt's face.

Disclaimer: The story, all names, characters, and incidents portrayed in this section are fictitious, Aunt _____. No identification with actual persons, places, buildings, and products is intended or should be inferred, Uncle _____. Please don't call my dad or threaten to disown me. Again. Love you, see you at Christmas!

Pace yourself. Family functions can be anxiety-inducing and overwhelming, even if you're not greeting fifty people every time you show up for a holiday. After hellos and hugs, it's tempting to beeline it to the bar and pour yourself a glass of whatever bottle of wine is open. I'm not going to deter you from that, because I do my best not to be a hypocrite, and lord knows I'm going to do just that every holiday for the rest of my life. But pace yourself, homie. You just walked in the door, and the cake won't be cut for a couple hours at least. No need to be six deep and trying to teach someone about intersectional feminism before you've finished your potato salad.

Keep the conversation light. Growing up, I was always

---

* The People's Elbow was one of the Rock's signature moves in the WWE before he Instagrammed his way into my heart. You should follow him. I followed him one day while drunk in an airport and it's honestly the only good decision I've ever made while drunk in an airport.

taught to never bring up politics or religion. And it's a pretty good rule when you're drinking with set-in-their-ways relatives, because those conversations are less like people talking and more like people throwing gasoline and matches at one another and setting the whole damn table on fire in the process. You're not convincing anyone of shit after having had a couple of glasses of wine, because for as passionate as you are to defend your stance on immigration, so is your uncle. Same with your super-religious aunt who is more likely to impale you with a butter knife than bend on abortion. With any conversation that you know is sparking a fuse rather than a genuine exchange of ideas, gently disengage and let them know you really need to go top off your Pinot Grigio.

I do genuinely believe in having hard conversations with your family, but do it soberly. I got into a huge argument with my father about Black Lives Matter one morning at 6:30 A.M., and I fought tooth and nail to get him to understand why I supported the movement. It was a hard conversation, but on the other side, I did end up teaching my father about BLM and he now understands the movement, and my support. I never want to discourage anyone from having conversations about important issues, especially with your family and friends, because I believe it is our responsibility to encourage the people around us to educate themselves on political and social issues. But trying to do it while drinking is likely to leave you and your family more divided and angry than before you started.

Do not under any circumstances bring up Facebook. Sure, it may start with you casually chirping about how adorable somebody's new kid is, but it will inevitably devolve into World War III over a fake news article. At least one person will be called a racist, and everyone will feel very awkward for a very long time.

Save the drama for your mama. Perhaps you've had a couple and your cousin Carrie is really getting on your nerves. Your whole life she's *alllllways* had to be better than you, and is *sooo* self-important, especially about this stupid new sales job, and remember that time . . . Nope. Stop it. Quit obsessing over dumb shit from years ago. No one remembers that thing she said when you guys were seven except you. Not only were you literal children and no one cares, but you probably are remembering it wrong anyway. Don't say shit to Carrie, and don't say shit to your other cousins about Carrie. Call your mom on the way home and complain about it like a civilized person who is most likely overreacting anyway.

Don't take shots with your cousins. Comradery is irresistible, especially when partnered with the bottle of Patrón your cousin Alec just happened to have in his backpack. But if you're on your third (be real, fourth) glass of wine, it's probably not in your best interest to start slinging shots with your younger counterparts. All right, fine. You can have *one*. Maybe two. OKAY, STOP, SERIOUSLY.

Stay in the open. You've been doing a wonderful job staying sane and totally together. Do not risk this lovely evening by letting yourself be cornered and asked one billion questions about when you're popping out some kids. Being berated in a corner about babies is a surefire way to tell a family member to fuck off, which I have found from personal experience does not go over well.

Get out before you're wasted. I don't care how you do

it. Lie, tell them you have work or a test or you have to take your dog to the dentist, doesn't matter. The only thing that matters is that you get out of there before you're too drunk and forget one of these many helpful hints. Get home safe and un-disowned, feeling very proud of yourself for not going apeshit on everyone for any number of reasons they most definitely gave you over the course of the evening.

You're Not Freaking Out Because of Zweigelt (or Any Other Wine)

Over the years, I've had a lot of people ask me what type of wine they should drink to "not freak out" at family functions. The thing is, wine isn't making you freak out at family functions. Your undealt-with issues are what's making you freak out. And that's okay! But if you have a hard time mixing wine and family, maybe it isn't the best idea to be drinking right now. Be honest with yourself. What is it that makes you freak out? Is it something you can let go of? Is it something you can talk to your family about (soberly) and resolve? Or is this something you should see a therapist about? Whatever the answers may be, it is in your best interest to work those out before drinking with your family again. Remember the ancient proverb, "Handle your shit or your shit will handle you."

HOW TO DRINK WITH YOUR BOSS & NOT LOSE YOUR JOB

Between happy hours, holiday parties, and hotel bars after the conference, there's a good chance you will find yourself drinking with your boss at some point. These can be some of the best times you'll ever have with your superiors, a chance to relax, get to know each other, and bond outside of the confines of a cubicle. Maybe even spit some wine knowledge. But no matter what type of relationship you have with your boss, no matter how awesome they are, getting drunk with your superiors is always precarious and should be approached cautiously. That harmless joke about ass play that's a hit with your coworkers may be a fireable offense after a few rounds with an executive you don't know very well outside of e-mail exchanges. At the end of the day, they're still your boss, and you want to keep it that way tomorrow.

Set a limit and stick to it. If you know you start to get loopy after two glasses of wine, make a promise to yourself that you're only having two glasses of wine. I know how fun drinking can be, and I know how easily two glasses turns into five, but it's not worth risking your reputation letting your superiors see the person your buddies call "Sir Pukes-A-Lot." You can also always set yourself an alarm for two hours into the future, title it "GET THE FUCK OUT BEFORE YOU EMBARRASS YOURSELF," and then do just that.

Don't talk shit. Everyone has coworkers they don't particularly like. When you're bro-ing down with your boss, you may feel comfortable enough to bring up how Jessica in accounting has been a total bitch lately, but don't. You don't know this person's relationship with your less-than-chill coworker, and it's more likely to hurt you than help. Even if they're not close with them, it makes you look unprofessional. If it's a real issue in the workplace, the conversation should be happening in the office, not over a bottle of rosé. And you shouldn't trust a boss that is down to shit-talk their employees with you either. If they're openly dishing all of Doug from design's dirt, chances are they have no problem talking about you in the same way.

Save talking about your raise for the office. Much like bringing up office drama, drinking with your boss is not the time to bring up that raise or promotion you've been waiting on. That is a conversation that needs to happen in the office, for both your sakes. They may have thrown back a couple and may be heaping on the praise, but you don't want an important conversation about your future to be a drunken conversation where everyone makes promises no one remembers to keep.

Don't get *too* personal. Getting to know people is one thing, and oversharing is another. This is my problem. Coming from comedy and building a career out of writing whatever I want, I'm not good at censoring myself. But the stuff I say onstage at a comedy club or to my friends isn't what I should be saying to my bosses. They don't need to know about the time I nearly broke my nose trying to seduce a dude by tripping and falling and hitting my face on his bed frame, nor do I need to joke about how I started going to therapy when I was ten. As much as we like to believe that people can separate business and personal, often people can't. You don't want your boss passing you in the hallway and thinking about that story you told about blowing your dude while watching *Jurassic Park* instead of that badass presentation you just crushed.

GO HOME. WHAT DID I TELL YOU? YOU ALREADY HAD TWO . . . OH, GODDAMN IT, THREE GLASSES, AND YOUR ALARM IS STILL GOING OFF. Go home, get a good night's sleep, and be back in the morning chipper as can be. Few things are more impressive than a person who keeps it professional over drinks and can wake up the next morning ready to get back to business. That raise is closer than ever!

HOW TO HAVE A SUCCESSFUL DRUNK HEART-TO-HEART

Sometimes you just need your friends, some open bottles of wine, a lot of hugs, and maybe even a good cry. Often you don't even plan these evenings; you just find yourself in the middle of them. While emotional support is something we all need from time to time, what no one needs is a drunken meltdown, which these sorts of events can easily become if you're not careful. Everyone has been there—the evening starts out fun and heartwarming, and it ends in eight bottles of wine and people screaming about how no one has the right to judge their relationships! Even if that significant other totally sucks and is the reason we needed to have a goddamn heart-to-heart to begin with! And then you have to have another heart-to-heart to fix everything from the last heart-to-heart.

Combining wine and feelings is as delicate and as temperamental as making a chocolate soufflé. When it's great, goddamn, is it great. And when it's bad, it is very bad and leaves everyone feeling deflated. Here's a recipe for success.

Have a specific number of bottles you're allotting for the evening. It's easy to get drinking, and drinking, and drinking some more. But drinking too much is never a good idea when you're dealing with feelings. You want to relax and loosen up, but you also want to remain calm, caring, and constructive, three words rarely used to describe anyone who is totally wasted. Get a couple of bottles and only open those. There are many more, less emotionally charged Saturday nights ahead of you to get together again if you're all really that fired up on drinking wine.

Eat. Because you know who is always the first one to throw a tantrum? The one who didn't eat but decided it was still a good idea to drink two bottles of wine. It's not a good idea. Ever!

Stay positive. When people are dealing with emotional stress, it is easy for them to become negative. Because alcohol is a depressant (another reason why no one should be drinking too much on nights like this), you want to steer conversations in positive directions. Pity parties never end well, so don't indulge people in their negativity. Always opt to look on the bright side, offer helpful advice, and be encouraging. If they're one of those people who becomes furious when people try to be positive when they're actively trying to be down in the dumps, just listen and be understanding. But still, do not promote negativity. It can spread throughout an entire evening, turning what could be an uplifting moment for friendship into a total bummer you just want to forget.

Don't mix drinks. If you finish your two bottles, don't let your friend bust out the vodka to keep going. While I've been known to have a few whiskeys amidst glasses of wine without a problem, you best believe if you've gone through multiple bottles and then start taking shots, you're going to have a bad time. Maybe not in that exact moment, but perhaps in an hour, and probably in the morning. Not only that, you don't want to promote using alcohol to escape life's problems. It's one thing to have a few glasses and vent, and it's another thing to actively try to black out and forget about a breakup. If someone starts hitting the bottle hard during an emotional time, please keep an eye on them and encourage healthier coping strategies.

Have some background noise. Ideally, it is a television show you and your friends love that is available for streaming, or that you have on DVD or Blu-ray or whatever the kids are using these days. That way it can be on all night while you talk over it from the couch. If shit gets a little too heavy or you're having a hard time steering away from negative waters, you can turn to the TV, laugh a little, and easily change the subject to how you wish you could build levels in your apartment like Kramer or how crazy it was that Carrie ever wore that dress made out of sewn-together bandanas with a cowboy hat.

Just be a good friend. That sounds simple, doesn't it? If only it were. It's not always easy to be there for people, nor are you always going to get the kind of love you want from people. Whether you're the one hugging or hurting, and maybe both, be kind and gentle with one another. Remember the golden rule: Bring wine. *I mean*, do unto others as you would have them do unto you. In this world, things like kindness and empathy are getting harder and harder to come by, and we all need more of it.

ACTIVITIES TO AVOID WHILE CONSUMING WINE

As your sage guide in your foray into wine, I believe it is not only my responsibility to teach you what you should do, but also what you should *not do* while consuming wine. What is one's life of drunken mistakes if not to be shared to help prevent others from doing the same dumb shit after two bottles of wine?

Don't drive. Never, ever, ever. Do not drink and drive. It's never been easier not to! Once upon a time it took hours to get a damn cab in Los Angeles; now it only takes three button pushes on the computer you keep in your pocket to get a car to come get you. It's so easy to think you're going to be the designated driver and then find yourself on your third drink, convincing yourself you're totally fine. Doesn't matter if you think you're fine, you can still be put in jail. I've never had a DUI, and that is in part because I make sure not to drive. Even when I only have $50 to my name, I am not driving if I know I'm drinking *anything*. You know how many people I know that got put in LA County jail for having two drinks and a broken taillight? Five! Being a little broke right now is way better than being $10,000 broker and everything else that comes along with getting arrested for drinking and driving. Please spend the extra $20 to get home safely.

Don't go to Zumba class. Especially not your first Zumba class. I don't know what the hell I was thinking, drinking half a bottle of $3 Cab before Zumba, but I suppose that's what being twenty-four is about, thinking you can do whatever you damn well please because you're old enough to be making decisions but young enough to believe you're indestructible. Usually, drinking makes me a better dancer, but it did not make me a better Zumba student, and it put my sweaty, heaving, wine-drunk existence face-to-face with its own mortality as I swung my limbs around like an uncoordinated primate. Needless to say, I did not return to Zumba (although to this day I am still on the studio's mailing list, as a quaint reminder not to be an idiot).

Don't cut your dog's hair. You may be asking why I would be cutting my dog's hair to begin with, and the answer is because I have some fluffy-ass dogs. I have to keep them trimmed up, unless I'd like to deal with some very messy situations. I've been trimming my dog Zissou's hair for a decade now, and I'm great at it. However, there was that one time that I drank more glasses of wine than I can count, and woke up with Zissou's backside looking like Freddy Krueger took a chain saw to the side of one of Edward Scissorhands's pristinely pruned topiaries. It was an embarrassing couple weeks for us all.

While we're at it, don't cut your own hair. I had bangs for fifteen years, bangs that I cut myself. And they were glorious! Internet-renowned, even! Ask anyone from the chillwave blog scene of the early 2010s! When my husband and I first started dating, he went away for Fourth of July. I stayed back in Los Angeles, and when he came home, he found that over the holiday I had cut my bangs about two inches above my eyebrows one night after having too much wine and alone time. I'm a perfectionist! They had to be even! Even if "even" meant trimming, and trimming, and trimming myself into extremely unflattering Bettie Page–style bangs that Ben later admitted made him wonder if we were going to work out.

Don't get into fights about how sexist _Game of Thrones_ is while you have company. When _GoT_ first came out, I fell asleep during an episode, only to wake up every time a woman was getting raped or was forced to eat a horse heart. This did not sit well with me. On one particular evening, we were having a small dinner party. A lot of wine had been consumed by the time _Game of Thrones_ came up, which everyone _loooved_. I said I hated it, because it was sexist and everyone was always getting raped. Ben said something along the lines of "Dude, you fall asleep in every episode, it's really not that bad. There are a lot of strong female characters." I refused to accept this, had a full meltdown at the table, and accused Ben—a journalism and ethnic studies double major, with certificates for his work in women's studies and a long history of activism—of hating women. No one at that dinner party has ever let me live this down, and to this day, I have not watched a single episode of _Game of Thrones_ because I am too prideful and refuse to admit I was maybe possibly wrong that one time I was drunk in 2011, even though _GoT_ went on to be the most talked-about TV show in my social circle and I may or may not have totally missed out and may or may not be a little bummed about it (or bummed that every time everyone comes over to watch it, I go sulk in my room and fuck around on Pinterest for an hour).

Don't shop online. This seems like a no-brainer. Who hasn't polished off a bottle of Riesling and is surprised two days later when Amazon has dropped off a package of pasties, an *Endless Summer* shower curtain, and a $100 fucking hairbrush? Totally normal. And while you shouldn't drink and shop online because you're probably blowing your cash on vintage telephones you can't even use because you don't even have a landline, I have another reason I don't buy stuff drunk on the Internet. Because one time I bought a bracelet I could not afford but had to have because I was drunk and it was limited edition and designed by my favorite blogger, the Coquette. Unfortunately, I failed to realize in my inebriated rush that I had it sent to my parents' address in my hometown that I had never deleted off my PayPal, which they had moved out of *five years ago*. I couldn't accept this as a loss; I couldn't accept tossing my money away and not having the bracelet. I ended up begging my grandmother to go knock on the door of my childhood home, and had to explain to her that I get drunk and buy things I can't afford, and she was very disappointed. And the only thing worse than disappointing your parents is disappointing your grandparents. So take this lesson and shop responsibly.

Don't talk about money with your partner. It never ends well. In fact, it usually ends with you sleeping on the couch to take a stand thinking your significant other will come out and get you, but instead, they fall asleep because it wasn't even a big deal to them, and now you're just angry on the couch for no reason.

Don't open that bottle of wine you've been saving. I know it's the last bottle you have, but you should not open it.

First of all, you're already drunk, otherwise we would not even be having this conversation. You're not going to even remember drinking it, let alone what it tastes like, and you're going to be bummed in the morning when you see its carcass on the counter amongst your empty LaCroix cans. Also: YOU CAN'T AFFORD TO REPLACE IT. DON'T OPEN IT! And while we're here, as a pro tip for the next time you're drunk and get a wise idea to say, "Fuck it, let's crack this super-rare Gut Oggau wine!" start putting sticky notes on your good wines that say, "DO NOT OPEN. SERIOUSLY. THIS IS REALLY GOOD WINE AND YOU'RE WASTED AND YOU'RE GOING TO REGRET THIS AND YOU'RE TOO POOR TO DRINK IT." That usually works. Even if you're not of sound mind, hopefully, someone with you will see the seriousness of the capital letters and talk you out of it.

Don't worry about it. IT'S WINE! It's for drinking! Much like sticky notes are for balling up and tossing in the trash like you're the Michael Jordan of Muscadet.

Of course, I want to drink wine all the time. I want to have fun and feel good and catch myself in fleeting moments of untouchable youth where time stands still just long enough for you to realize you are truly free. Not in an "I'm popping Molly at Coachella!" way. That is seriously the last thing in the whole fucking world I want to do, second only to popping Molly at Stagecoach, an actual circle of hell. But in a genuine living-in-the-moment type of way, where you're so present that even for a split second, all that matters is the company around you, that glass in front of you, and the feeling of endless happiness in those few minutes.

Drinking in the real world is balancing the pursuit of good times with being a responsible human. Wine is the most pleasurable thing on the planet, but not if you're setting shit on fire at family functions or chugging bottles in the park around families with piñatas and eventually the police. Always be mindful of those around you, your environment, and your own well-being. By approaching drinking with this consideration, you can create a sustainable lifestyle of wine times that will enhance your experiences well into your grandpa years (when you can throw consideration out the door and do whatever the hell you please).

To-Drink List:

1. I don't want to encourage you to break any laws, but next time you want to take wine with you, DO IT DO IT DO IT! *Responsibly!*

2. Practice setting limits for yourself, whether you're out with your boss or anyone. It's incredible how useful it can be to say you need to go home—even if you're having a great time and your friends are begging you to continue the party somewhere else—and stick to it.

3. Whip up some kalimotxos one weekend. THEY ARE REALLY GOOD, I SWEAR!

Outro

I feel like the music has come on and I am being played off the stage, trying to rush through the fifteen-minute speech I wrote for a thirty-second spot. I feel like I have so much more to tell you, and I feel like we've only just begun.

And that's because we have.

Wine is an ocean of a subject, deep and expansive.

We just did a day trip, snorkeling on vacation in it.

And I hope you had a good time.

I hope you feel inspired to drink new wines you're not afraid to try, or buy, or order. I hope you feel excited to have your friends over to share a bottle, share some stories, and share your newfound wine knowledge. I hope you feel like the confident wine drinker I promised you would be.

Because you are.

You have everything you need.

Now you just have to believe it, and get out there and drink some wine.

Cheers,

Marissa Ross

MAR

PS: The hangover cure is water, weed, Coca-Cola, pizza, and/or burrito, repeat. Godspeed! xox

Acknowledgments

They say it takes a village to raise a kid, but it also takes one to write a book, and I would like to take this moment to thank all the wonderful people who had a hand in making this book happen.

First, my incredible agent and friend, Rachel Vogel of Waxman Leavell. In Los Angeles, the words "agent" and "friend" are rarely in the same sentence, but Rachel goes above and beyond each of those titles. The first time we spoke, I was on the phone in my car in Mindy Kaling's driveway while the DirecTV guy knocked on the window and I begged him to please wait because this was the biggest call of my life. She heard the entire conversation and *still* took me seriously. She believed in me when few were willing to give me a chance, has guided me through one of the most complex projects and experiences of my life with warmth and consideration, and has dealt with more of my existential crises than any human I'm not paying or sleeping with should. She's the best.

Second, my badass editor Kate Napolitano at Plume. We had tried to meet twice before my proposal was even done, and both times we entirely missed each other with mixed-up dates and times. Third time truly was a charm; we shared some wine, had some laughs, and if this had been a first date, it would have been one of those first dates where you're one hundred percent convinced you're going to marry that person. She just got it. She sculpted this book without stripping away any of my voice or vision, and for that, along with her hard work, invaluable insight, and support, I am forever grateful.

I've been so fortunate to be surrounded by some of the most talented and generous people in wine, and I owe them many thanks. Kashy Khaledi, proprietor of Ashes & Diamonds Winery in Napa, has been an honorary older brother to me since I started my *Wine Time* videos in 2011. Not only did he introduce me to so much wine, history, and appreciation, but he has never stopped pushing me to be better and learn more. Jill Bernheimer of Domaine LA, Lou Amdur of Lou Wine Shop, Silverlake Wine, and their staffs over the years have been instrumental and vital in my growth as a wine drinker and writer. Without their shops, knowledge, and kindness, I wouldn't drink nearly as well as I do. Distributors and importers like Amy Atwood of Amy Atwood Selections and Cory Cartwright of Selection Massale have also played a huge part in my life in wine, and, of course, the many huge-hearted winemakers they represent. No one had to be nice or welcoming to some random girl with a blog, but they were, especially winemakers here in my home state of California.

My sister, Valerie, is my everything, and I wouldn't be anywhere without her limitless love and encouragement. I would need to write a whole other book to simply scratch the surface of how important she is to me. Valerie has been cheering me on (and putting up with me) since I was hosting comedy shows from our family's fireplace when we were kids. She is my rock, my sounding board, my best friend, and my monkey. She has also seen every headshot I've ever taken and still loves me, so you know it's real.

I would also like to thank all my friends and family who have been there for me before, and throughout, this project. Especially my parents, Dave and Gail. My father gave me my ambition, my mother never let me stop dreaming, and they both gave me the strength and confidence to pursue my passion even when I was told it would be impossible. Special thank-you to the homie/the only sommelier I could trust to read this over without killing me, Adam Vourvoulis, and extra fist bumps to my best bro and temp research assistant, E. Ryan Ellis.

Despite already dedicating this book to him, there is no one that deserves more thanks than my extraordinary husband, Benjamin Blascoe. None of this would be possible without him. He believed in me when I was a cocky college dropout with big dreams and no practical plans. He believed in me when I was a struggling writer with three day jobs and a blog no one read. He believed in me when I was given a chance. More specifically, he put on Van Halen's "Jump" and convinced me to quit my job and write the proposal for this book.

From the moment we met, I promised you I'd make it.

But now that I'm here, it's more than that.

We made it.

Index

Note: Page numbers in **bold** indicate glossary terms.
Page numbers in parentheses indicate noncontiguous references.